Global Interest in Student Behavior

Global Interest in Student Behavior

An Examination of International Best Practices

Charles J. Russo, Izak Oosthuizen,
and Charl C. Wolhuter

ROWMAN & LITTLEFIELD
Lanham • Boulder • New York • London

Published by Rowman & Littlefield
A wholly owned subsidiary of The Rowman & Littlefield Publishing Group, Inc.
4501 Forbes Boulevard, Suite 200, Lanham, Maryland 20706
www.rowman.com

Unit A, Whitacre Mews, 26-34 Stannery Street, London SE11 4AB

Copyright © 2015 by Charles J. Russo, Izak Oosthuizen, and Charl C. Wolhuter

British Library Cataloguing in Publication Information Available

Library of Congress Cataloging-in-Publication Data

Russo, Charles J.
Global interest in student behavior : an examination of international best practices / Charles J. Russo;
Izak Oosthuizen and Charl C. Wolhuter.
p. cm.
Includes bibliographical references
ISBN 978-1-4758-1479-8 (cloth) -- ISBN 978-1-4758-1480-4 (pbk.) -- ISBN 978-1-4758-1481-1
(electronic)
1. Classroom management. 2. Behavior modification--Cross-cultural studies. 3. Problem children--
Behavior modification--Cross-cultural studies. 4. Behavior disorders in children--Cross-cultural stud-
ies. I. Oosthuizen, Izak. II. Wolhuter, C. C. (Charl C.) III. Title.
LB3011.R77 2014
371.102'4--dc23
                                                                                    2014042794

To our wives,
Debbie
Amori
Irené
With all of our love and affection

Contents

Preface

A cornerstone for effective teaching and learning is vested in the quality of the way in which students focus on the content of their lessons.[1] Educational practitioners and academics agree that classroom order is a *sine qua non* for effective learning. A constant challenge for teachers and other educational leaders in seeking to maintain safe and orderly learning environments is the seemingly endless occurrences of student misconduct. Moreover, there appears to be a worldwide deterioration of student conduct in schools.

As the world becomes a global village, educators can learn from the experiences of colleagues in other nations who have had success in addressing issues of student discipline. Consequently, it is important for practitioners to uncover effective methods to deal with student misconduct. The objective of this book, then, is to identify the best practices in ten nations on six continents for dealing with student misconduct in a legally sound manner.

It is a well-accepted and tested practice that when national education systems grapple with educational issues, comparative-international perspectives can be reviewed for assistance. Put another way, when countries face particular educational issues or challenges, educators in one nation could benefit from the experience of their peers elsewhere who faced or are still facing similar concerns. The study of the experience of educators in other countries can reveal the full extent and implications of the problem and possible contributory causes while suggesting solutions for dealing with student misconduct. Against this background this volume offers the experience of ten countries in dealing with student misconduct in the hopes that it will open a wider perspective to academics, policy makers, and educators alike, eventually making a contribution toward the successful dealing with student misconduct.

The chapters in this book offer cross-national perspectives on best practices when dealing with the challenge of student misconduct. The chapter authors, all distinguished academics or jurists, have contributed their reviews of the state of the law and practice in their nations. As readers peruse the chapters, they will recognize that the way in which educators address student discipline varies around the world.

As such, this is the fifth book in a series of volumes on comparative legal issues in education. The earlier volumes addressed the rights of students,[2] teachers,[3] and students with disabilities,[4] in addition to the status of higher education.[5] The chapters on individual countries in this volume are Australia (Joan Squelch), Brazil (Nina Beatriz Stocco Ranieri), China (Ran Zhang, Jun Wang, and Suping Shen), Malaysia (Fatt Hee Tie), New Zealand (Sally Varnham), Singapore (Mui Kim Teh), South Africa (Marius H. Smit and J. P. Rossouw), Turkey (Ricardo Lozano and Irem Kizilaslan), United Kingdom (Patricia Walker), and United States (Charles J. Russo). The book rounds out with a chapter of analysis by the editors that draws on the issues raised throughout the book and centers on the concept of best practice management, ending with concrete suggestions aimed at improving educational practice.

The first book of its kind, and a companion volume to the comparative texts identified earlier, consists of a collection of chapters designed to enhance a common understanding of the rights of students when they are subjected to discipline. As the world continues to shrink, and interdependence grows, a major challenge facing educators in the global community is ensuring the rights of students who are being disciplined while working to maintain order so that their other children can learn in safe and orderly school environments.

Readers are advised that insofar as each of the nations covered in this book uses slightly different systems of legal citation, we have left references in their original form rather than attempt to standardize them under one American rubric. Finally, we preserved minor variations in the different forms of English used globally so that readers can get a flavor of how this seemingly common tongue is used throughout the world, particularly for academics whose native language is not English.

Of course, no single book can ever hope to cover the myriad of legal topics, or laws of nations, addressing the legal status of discipline in schools. Even so, we hope that these informative, thought provoking, well-written, and researched chapters, authored by leading academics or jurists in the field, can serve as up-to-date and ready sources of information to help keep educational leaders, academics, and students abreast of the many changes in the ever-growing area of comparative student discipline.

NOTES

1. For the sake of consistency, this book usually refers to children in K–12 schools as students. Even so, the authors recognize that other nations use different terms. For example, educators in South Africa tend to speak of "learners," while those in the United Kingdom typically refer to "pupils." Thus, we have left these variations in place rather than seek to standardize the use of terminology.

2. Charles J. Russo, Jan DeGroof, and Douglas J. Stewart, eds., *The Educational Rights of Students: International Perspectives on Demystifying the Legal Issues* (Lanham, MD: Rowman and Littlefield Education, 2007).

3. Charles J. Russo and Jan DeGroof, eds., *The Employment Rights of Teachers: Exploring Education Law Worldwide* (Lanham, MD: Rowman and Littlefield Education, 2009).

4. Charles J. Russo, ed., *The Legal Rights of Students with Disabilities: International Perspectives* (Lanham, MD: Rowman and Littlefield Education, 2011).

5. Charles J. Russo, ed., *Handbook of Comparative Higher Education Law* (Lanham, MD: Rowman and Littlefield Education, 2011).

Acknowledgments

As with any book, there are a number of people who must be thanked. Four sets of people were very helpful in putting this book together. First, many thanks to Tom Koerner, vice president and editorial director at Rowman and Littlefield Education, who was most supportive of this project from its inception through publication. Thanks also to Carlie Wall, associate editor, Chris Basso, production editor, and Crystal Clifton for copyediting the text.

Second, it almost goes without saying that we are grateful to the authors for their valuable contributions to this book.

Third, we would like to thank Charlie's assistant, Elizabeth Pearn at the University of Dayton for her efforts in copyediting and helping to prepare the final manuscript for publication.

Fourth, but certainly not least, we would like to express our deepest appreciation for our wives, Debbie, Amori, and Irené, to whom this book is dedicated, for their ongoing love and support, without which none of this work would have been completed.

Introduction

The objective of this first volume of companion books on student discipline is to identify the best practices in dealing with student misconduct on six continents in a legally sound manner. It is essential for educators to examine national as well as international practices addressing student misconduct in schools because learner misbehavior often has a detrimental effect on the quality of teaching and learning in elementary and secondary schools.

The essence of order in school environments can hardly be overemphasized. In the context of teaching-learning, order is to be regarded as a *sine qua non* (an indispensable condition) for effective learning. One of the cornerstones for effective teaching and learning is vested in the extent to which students can focus on the content of lessons. Interruptions as a result of student noise such as talking during lessons, or when learners constantly interrupt teachers can upset the focus of an entire class.

These companion volumes are designed to show how learner misconduct calls for global awareness and collaboration. It is important to study this issue because not only are everyday trivial disturbances in class problems, but from media reports incidents of serious misconduct are increasing. In fact, there have been multiple assaults and killing of learners and teachers on school premises. Moreover, the latter constitute more than mere misconduct, they are acts of criminal misbehavior.

When student misbehavior turns into serious misconduct and ultimately criminal activity, alarms sound in the global community insofar as schools have sadly become danger zones instead of secure, tranquil environments enhancing teaching and learning. It is thus time to rethink strategies and approaches to learner discipline.

Educators can effectively learn from the experiences of peers in other countries, especially from their successes dealing with student misconduct.

As such, this book endeavors to promote a global reciprocity as it examines causes, tendencies, and forms of misconduct in ten nations. Further, this book focuses on effective methods of dealing with student misconduct.

Following this brief introduction, which highlights key themes to be identified, the remainder of the book analyzes the detrimental effects student misconduct is having on teaching and learning environments in schools.

MISCONDUCT HAMPERS TEACHING AND LEARNING

A constant encumbrance for order in teaching and learning environments is student misconduct. The Teaching and Learning International Survey, *Creating Effective Teaching and Learning Environments: First Results*, by the Organization for Economic Cooperation and Development (OECD Report),[1] highlighted international concern for studying the detrimental effects student misconduct is having on teaching and learning. The OECD report contained a comprehensive survey of ninety thousand teachers in twenty-three countries.

One of the findings of the OECD Report was that although positive school climates were associated with higher levels of student achievement, disruption of class instruction due to learner misconduct hinders the provision of proper instruction. As such, these disruptions have detrimental effects on teaching and learning.

In addition to disturbances in the classrooms, which ranked first among the incidences of misconduct, the OECD Report ranked the other high frequented incidences of student misconduct as student absenteeism (46 percent); students arriving late at school (39 percent); profanity and swearing (37 percent); intimidation or verbal abuse of other students (35 percent); intimidation and verbal abuse of teachers and staff (17 percent); physical injury of other students (16 percent); theft (15 percent); and possession of alcohol or drugs (11 percent).[2]

CONCERN FOR STUDENT SAFETY

Another important aspect which necessitates the proper handling of student misconduct refers to the safety of fellow learners and school staff. It is important that teachers respond immediately to minor incidents of misconduct before they can escalate into more serious difficulties that can pose a threat to the safety of school communities.

THE PROBLEM OF CRIMINAL TENDENCIES

It is critical that some forms of serious misconduct, such as the possession of drugs or weapons and assaults on teachers or peers, are criminal offenses. In perhaps the two worst examples of such behavior, at Columbine High School in Colorado and in Sandy Hook Elementary School in Newtown, Connecticut,[3] students went so far as attacking and killing other learners and peers. It goes without saying that tendencies such as these cannot be ignored or go unpunished since remaining passive in the face of such behavior would actually be the same as condoning it. Further, tolerating these tendencies would constitute professional negligence.

DEALING WITH MISCONDUCT

In numerous schools worldwide, there appears to be a need for additional, legally sound methods to deal with student misconduct more effectively. Traditional methods applicable to typical student misconduct such as detention, the setting of school and classroom rules, demerit points, and corporal punishment (in some countries) are effectively applied in some situations but in others they prove to be less effective.

Many educational practitioners claim that the majority of these traditional methods are less effective while others argue that the application of corporal punishment proves to be one of the most effective methods in dealing with learner misconduct. Yet, in many countries corporal punishment in schools is regarded as unconstitutional or deemed to be inhuman and degrading.

Dealing with Serious Misconduct

A major problem actually lies with the serious forms of student misconduct. This leads to the following questions:

- How should teachers deal with serious forms of misconduct?
- What methods are available to deal effectively with student violence, theft, assault, and possession of drugs or dangerous weapons?
- What methods are utilized in ten countries on the six inhabited continents?
- Which of these methods are applied effectively?
- What other possible methods can be suggested or should be developed?

THE GLOBAL JOURNEY

In the quest to find answers to these questions, this book embarks on a tour through the global village. The remainder of this chapter provides a brief overview of dealing with learner misconduct in Australia, New Zealand, Singapore, the United Kingdom, and the United States.

In Australia there appears to be a strong emphasis on the creation of safe school environments based on government initiatives. Consequently, Australian schools are generally regarded as safe and orderly places.

Among others nations, bullying is a concern in schools in New Zealand. Since reactive and retributive disciplinary methods from the past showed little success, educational authorities of the country decided to change their approach by adopting more restorative oriented strategies. This paved the way for approaches embedded in initiatives evidenced by *Respectful Schools: Restorative Practices in Education* of 2007. This report endeavored to set schools on a road toward restorative practices with an eye toward changing school cultures founded on value systems of support, repair, reintegration, and inclusion of all.

The 1980s and 1990s pattern of trivial incidents of student misconduct in Singaporean schools is shifting. As of late, more serious forms of learner misconduct (and even forms of crime) are emerging, a tendency some blame on media reports of school shootings and bullying in the United Kingdom and United States.

Against this background, there is a strong thrust toward interventions assisting students with behavioral problems. The Response, Early Interventions and Assessment in Company Mental Health or REACH Program, launched in 2007, deals with behavioral problems of learners in Singapore. This initiative consists of relying on multidisciplinary teams of medical doctors, clinical psychologists, medical social workers, and nurses working with students.

In 2011, the Office for Standards in Education, commonly referred to as Ofsted, reported that the conduct of students in the United Kingdom is not better than satisfactory. As to secondary schools, the findings rated learner conduct in 18.4 percent of schools to be only satisfactory or inadequate. On the other hand, primary schools were rated high: in 37.9 percent of schools the conduct was adjudged as outstanding; good in 55.8 percent; below good in 6.2 percent; and inadequate in only 0.1 percent of cases. Various forms of bullying appear to be one of the main problems as it was reported that about 20 percent of UK children are victimized by cyber-bullying. Measures officials use when dealing with serious pupil misconduct are referrals, restorative justice, mediation, internal exclusions, and managed moves to another school.

The quest for democracy in a fair and just society in the United States, directed to matters concerning the constitutional rights of students, paved the way for a myriad of litigation beginning in the late 1960s. Although this upsurge of litigation was often characterized by contradiction and some issues remain unresolved, the cases established constitutional essentials regarding a fair and just dispensation in dealing with learner conduct.

As a result of more than fifty years of litigation on student rights, the United States has established a suitable foundation for human rights serving as a model for schools in the civilized world. To this end, the U.S. Supreme Court's 1975 judgment in *Goss v. Lopez*,[4] which examined the essentials of due process in schools, is regarded by many as the *Magna Carta* of student rights and deemed worthy of being emulated.

CONCLUSION

The sound management of learner misconduct is essential for optimal teaching and learning. In many instances schools and societies lost track in dealing with learner misconduct to the detriment of orderly teaching and learning environments. In other settings it appears that school officials found the key to enhance positive student conduct to the best interest of the young.

All who are interested in education should seek to capture some of these successful strategies for application in their own challenging circumstances. The global overview of learner conduct in the following chapters provides a window of opportunity for reciprocity, thereby creating an option to exchange the pages from one another's experiences.

NOTES

1. Available at http://www.oecd.org/edu/school/43023606.pdf (OECD Report). See also http://www.oecd.org/edu/school/creatingeffectiveteachingandlearningenvironmentsfirstresults-fromtalis.htm.

2. Id. at 40.

3. For a commentary on this tragedy, see Charles J. Russo. "Armed Teachers and Guards Won't Make Schools Safer." *Education Week* 32(19) (2013): 27, 32.

4. 419 U.S. 565 (1975).

Chapter One

School Discipline and the Law in Australia

Joan Squelch

Before reviewing issues associated with school discipline in Australia, it is helpful to understand how its legal system operates. In 1901 the Commonwealth of Australia was established as a federation under the *Commonwealth of Australia Constitution Act 1900* (the Australian Constitution), an Act of the Parliament of the United Kingdom. [1]

The Commonwealth of Australia is made up of six states and two mainland self-governing territories. The six self-governing states are New South Wales, Queensland, South Australia, Tasmania, Victoria, and Western Australia each with their own constitution. The two self-governing territories are the Australian Capital Territory (ACT) and the Northern Territory. [2]

Under the Australian federal system of government, each of the nine jurisdictions, including the Commonwealth, has three branches of government: the executive or administrative, judiciary or courts, and legislature or parliament. [3] A feature of the federal system is that the Australian Constitution provides for lawmaking powers to be shared between the Commonwealth Parliament and the parliaments of the states. [4] While exclusive powers are enumerated matters over which only the Commonwealth Parliament can enact valid laws, concurrent powers that are identified in section 51 of the Constitution, list matters [5] over which both the Commonwealth and states can enact valid laws. [6]

Residual matters, those not specifically provided for in the Australian Constitution, fall within the wide lawmaking powers of the states. [7] Education falls within the residual lawmaking powers of the states. States have their own Constitutions under which they have plenary powers to make laws for "the peace, order and good government" of the state. [8] Therefore, the states have full power to legislate over matters relating to education, which provides the legal basis for school management and discipline. Each state therefore has its own legal framework for the provision and administration of schools, including school discipline and behavior management.

THE AUSTRALIAN SCHOOL SYSTEM

Under the federal system of government, each Australian state and territory is mainly responsible for its own education system and for the provision, governance, control, and funding of state education.[9] The system of schooling in all jurisdictions includes government or state schools and non-government or private schools.[10]

State and territory governments provide some funding to non-government schools, but the Commonwealth Government is the main source of public funding for non-government schools. Although largely autonomous, non-government schools are required to be registered, and are subject to state laws and regulations.[11]

Formal schooling generally lasts for twelve years and comprises six to seven years of primary schooling and five to six years of secondary schooling. School attendance in Australia is compulsory for children between the ages of six and sixteen but may vary between states and territories.[12]

Education Administration

The education system in each jurisdiction is administered by a department of education overseen by a Minister of Education and a Director General (or in some jurisdictions a Secretary of Education) who is the Chief Executive Officer and the person responsible to the Minister for the overall operation of education. The powers and functions of education Ministers and Chief Executive Officers are set out in respective state and territory education legislation.[13] Chief Executive Officers, who are subject to the control and direction of the Minister, perform functions or exercise powers that the Minister is authorized or required to perform or exercise under the respective education legislation.[14]

Ministerial functions, and those exercised by a CEO or Director General on the instruction of the Minister, are generally broad and include functions relating to establishing, maintaining, and closing schools and education services; allocating resources, including providing financial assistance to non-government schools; exempting children from attending school; approving programs of instruction; establishing school councils; granting or refusing applications for home education; and registering and controlling nongovernment schools. Importantly, a primary function includes excluding students from school; controlling discipline; and establishing guidelines for school codes of conduct.

School Management

School principals, or head teachers, are responsible for the day-to-day operations and management of primary and secondary schools. Key functions of principals are to provide educational leadership and management of their schools; contribute to the development and implementation of educational policies and strategies; ensure that instruction provided in their school is in accordance with relevant curriculum policy; ensure the safety and welfare of students; and promote cooperation with their local communities.[15]

A primary function of school principals is to oversee the development, administration, implementation, and monitoring of school discipline, which is essential for creating and maintaining safe and productive learning environments. All schools are required to have behavior management plans for students.[16]

In Western Australia, for instance, principals of government schools are responsible for the day-to-day management and control of their school, including all persons on school premises and have the "duty to ensure the safety and welfare of students on the school premises and away from the school premises but on school activities, so far as that can reasonably be done."[17]

School principals may also give directions, either generally or in specific cases, concerning the procedures to be observed by persons on school premises to manage and control the school and persons thereon; to maintain good order on school premises; and to ensure the safety and welfare of persons on the premises.[18]

School Councils

All state schools have school councils to assist with the governance of schools. The roles and responsibilities of school councils are also set out in the respective state and territory education legislation or regulations.[19] The legal status and responsibilities of school councils may vary across the states and territories. In some states, councils are mandatory and have a high degree of decision-making powers while in others they are optional with varying levels of decision-making powers.

In Victoria, by way of illustration, all schools are governed by school councils that are legal entities incorporated under part 2.3 of the *Education and Training Reform Act 2006* (Vic). In Western Australia,[20] South Australia,[21] and the ACT,[22] which has school boards, school councils are also mandatory. In Western Australia, though, education legislation also allows for councils to become incorporated;[23] both incorporated and unincorporated councils may apply to the Minister to extend their functions under section 129 of the *School Education Act 1999* (WA).[24]

In Tasmania, state schools must have school associations[25] while in the Northern Territory, the Minister may, at the request of interested bodies involved in the management of state schools or from the communities served by state schools, establish school councils.[26] In New South Wales[27] and Queensland,[28] government schools may establish councils but insofar as there is no mandatory requirement, they have limited decision-making powers.

School councils play an important role in schools, in general. Even so, councils in all states are advisory with limited powers. Councils are not directly involved in the day-to-day operation and management of schools; this duty is the responsibility of principals. Nonetheless, councils have a responsibility to help develop, monitor, and review codes of conduct or behavior management plans for students. Councils generally provide guidance on the strategic direction and priorities of schools; help to develop and review school policies; monitor school performance; encourage parental involvement; and ensure the efficient and effective use of resources.[29]

POSITIVE SCHOOL DISCIPLINE AND SAFE SCHOOLS: GUIDING PRINCIPLES

School safety and the promotion of positive discipline, in addition to the effective management of student behavior, are high priorities for education departments and school officials. In Australia, the framing and implementation of education law and policy are underpinned by guiding principles advocating and supporting proactive, positive, and educative approaches to discipline and behavior management that give effect to the fundamental rights of children and freedoms such as to learn in safe environment free from disruptions, intimidation, harassment, and discrimination.[30]

The Queensland code of conduct for school behavior, for example, declares that schools are "committed to providing quality learning opportunities that enable all students to achieve within safe, supportive and disciplined learning environments" and that "essential to effective learning is a safe, supportive and disciplined environment that respects the rights of all students to learn, the rights of teachers to teach and the rights of all to be safe."[31]

In Tasmania, the aims of school discipline policies include "to protect the rights of the students, staff and learning community"; "to safeguard the right of teachers to be able to teach without unacceptable disruption"; and "to safeguard the right of students to learn without unacceptable disruption."[32]

The New South Wales policy on student discipline in government schools likewise directs that "all students and staff have the right to be treated fairly and with dignity in an environment free from disruption, intimidation, harassment, victimization and discrimination."[33] To achieve these goals, all Australian schools are expected to maintain high standards of discipline and safety as well as to have effective policies and procedures in place to promote safe, orderly schools.

The ongoing development and implementation of policies and practices based on principles of best practice is given further impetus by the National Safe Schools Framework (NSSF), which was launched in 2003 with the aim of providing a set of common principles for establishing safe and supportive school environments. The NSSF was established by the Ministerial Council on Education, Employment, Training, and Youth Affairs as a collaborative effort by the Commonwealth Government, state and territory governments, nongovernment school authorities, and various other key stakeholders.[34]

The revised NSSF is based on the vision that "[a]ll Australian schools are safe, supportive and respectful teaching and learning communities that promote student wellbeing."[35] The NSSF describes a safe and supportive school as follows: "[i]n a safe and supportive school, the risk from all types of harm is minimized, diversity is valued and all members of the school community feel respected and included and can be confident that they will receive support in the face of any threats to their safety or wellbeing."[36]

The NSSF sets out nationally agreed to principles for safe and supportive environments which include implementing policies, programs, and processes to nurture safe and supportive school environments while taking action to protect children from all forms of abuse and neglect.[37] The NSSF therefore provides an important basis on which to develop and implement comprehensive, coherent, and systematic school policies and procedures to effectively manage school discipline, with a view to continuous improvement.

SCOPE OF STATUTORY SCHOOL DISCIPLINE STRATEGIES

Australia is not generally associated with violence in schools and excessive antisocial behavior; however, school officials are nonetheless faced with the challenge of managing student behavior and various types of misconduct that may range from minor breaches of school rules to more serious forms of antisocial conduct and criminal offences such as school bullying, physical assaults on students and teachers, and property destruction.

No comprehensive research or data are available on the range and frequency of the types of misconduct in schools; anecdotally, typical forms of misconduct include:

- less serious breaches of school policies and rules such as arriving late for school, minor class disruptions, and minor acts of insubordination
- fighting
- minor theft
- vandalism
- bullying[38]
- truancy
- possession of dangerous weapons
- possession of illegal drugs or other substances

Teachers may implement a wide range of appropriate classroom management strategies to effectively create and manage safe, orderly, and disciplined learning environments. In addition, in all Australian jurisdictions certain disciplinary methods and procedures for dealing with misconduct are found in relevant state legislation and regulations, in particular matters relating to corporal punishment, suspension, and expulsion.[39]

The statutory methods are aimed at dealing with more serious forms of misconduct and disruptions to the learning environment, and conduct that threatens the safety of others such as bullying and acts of violence. Other strategies including detention, time-out, and community or school service are also provided for in state legislation and regulations. While approaches to discipline vary from jurisdiction to jurisdiction, there is much common ground in terms of the legal scope and procedures for implementing these methods.

Corporal Punishment

Corporal punishment, which has been defined as "the application of force to cause pain,"[40] is prohibited in schools in Australia other than the Northern Territory. This prohibition is not expressly provided for in all legislation, though.

Since the 1990s, corporal punishment has been phased out in Australian schools, even though under criminal codes reasonable corporal punishment is not a criminal offense in some states. Legislation in New South Wales,[41] Tasmania,[42] and Victoria[43] states that corporal punishment is not permitted in government and nongovernment schools, while the ACT[44] bans corporal punishment in "schools," which on interpretation applies to government and nongovernment schools.

In Western Australia,[45] corporal punishment is banned in government schools, but this does not extend to nongovernment schools. In Queensland and South Australia legislation does not specifically deal with corporal punishment but corporal punishment has been abolished in both states. However, in Queensland, an old law dating back to 1899 on domestic punishment still makes it lawful "for a parent or person in the place of a parent, or for a school teacher or master to use, by way of correction, discipline, management or control, towards a child or pupil, under the person's care, such force as is reasonable under the circumstances."[46]

In the Northern Territory no express provision bans corporal punishment in legislation; however, section 11 of the Criminal Code Act provides that "a person who may justifiably apply force to a child for the purposes of discipline, management or control" and, "where that other person is a school teacher of the child," it shall be presumed that the power has been delegated unless it is expressly withheld."

The issue of corporal punishment raises the question about the use of "reasonable force" or "restraint" to discipline children. Education laws and policies recognize the use of reasonable force or restraint "as an immediate or emergency response"[47] to protect the student concerned and prevent the student from placing others at risk or damaging property.

New South Wales education legislation, for example, defines corporal punishment as "the application of physical force in order to punish or correct the student, but does not include the application of force only to prevent personal injury to, or damage to or the destruction of property of, any person (including the student)."[48] Similarly, in Victorian schools, a staff member of a government school may take "any reasonable action that is immediately required to restrain a student of the school from acts or behaviour dangerous to the member of staff, the student or any other person."[49]

School and Community Service

Some jurisdictions include school and community service as a permissible discipline method. For example, New South Wales guidelines and codes may permit "other reasonable forms of punishment or correction of those students" including requiring "students to perform any reasonable work or service for the school."[50]

Detention

Detention is a permissible form of discipline in all Australian jurisdictions, the authority of which may be found in legislation, departmental guidelines, or local school policies.[51] Tasmanian legislation, for instance, allows school principals to impose detention if "satisfied that a student has behaved in an unacceptable manner."[52] Detention is considered an "appropriate level of response for much irresponsible classroom behavior" and that it "signals to a student that irresponsible behaviour which breaks class rules or school rules will be met with an immediate consequence."[53]

The Tasmanian Department of Education defines "detention" as any relatively short period when a student is detained at school, or in a particular class, in a student's "nonclass" time such as during recess, lunchtime, recreation time, or after school or excluded from normal classes, or from a particular class, pending negotiated conditions for reentry (time-out). [54]

In South Australia, teachers may "detain a student during the luncheon interval or after school hours subject to any conditions determined by the Minister."[55] Similarly, in Western Australia teachers or principals may detain students but for no longer than thirty minutes. The regulations further require principals to "take all reasonable steps" to contact the persons lawfully responsible for the students *and* to ensure that arrangements are in place for the students to get home. [56]

Where detention is used, the following guidelines apply to ensure student safety and that students do not miss work: [57]

- Detentions must be supervised by a member of the teaching staff.
- Where students are detained at school before or after normal school hours, it may be necessary to notify their parents or the persons lawfully responsible for their welfare.
- If detention is imposed after school, arrangements must be made to ensure the student's safe transport home.
- The guidelines for detentions should be made explicitly in the school's discipline policy.

Time-Out Strategies

Australian schools are permitted to use "time-out" as a strategy to reinforce positive behavior. [58] Time-out is defined "as giving a student time away from their regular class program/routine: to a separate area within classroom or to another supervised room or setting."[59] Generally, time-out rooms must be suitable and provide adequate space, and students must be engaged in meaningful educational activities and be supervised at all times. [60]

The New South Wales Department of Education provides an example of good practice policy to ensure that time-out is one of various interventions "used to assist students to regulate and/or control their behaviour. It is used as a proactive strategy to support self-calming and to provide an opportunity for students to reflect on their actions."[61] It is also required that "time-out strategies are not to be used as punishment or as a means of removing students indefinitely from the classroom" and that "it is a means of calming students during a stressful situation within a safe and predictable environment."[62]

Suspension, Exclusion, and Expulsion

Each Australian jurisdiction has legislative provisions, regulations, departmental policies, and school policies dealing with suspensions, exclusions, and expulsions that vary from one jurisdiction to the next. Given the extent of variations across the jurisdictions, it is necessary to consult each of the relevant state and territory laws and policies. However, for the purpose of this chapter, an overview of general principles and approaches is provided with regard to the power to exclude students, the grounds for exclusion, and the procedures that must be followed.

The main distinction between suspension, exclusion, and expulsion is the length of time students are excluded from school. Suspensions generally refer to the temporary removal, whether full time or part time, of students from school for specified periods of time (usually ten days) while expulsions are permanent removals. Some jurisdictions also include the category of exclusion, the temporary removal of students from school for longer periods of time (usually more than ten days).[63] While the duration of removal varies, typically short suspensions are up to five consecutive days and no more than fifteen days during the school year and no more than four times in a year.

Exclusion, or longer suspensions, may be for a period longer than two weeks and up to twenty days in some jurisdictions (e.g., New South Wales). In Western Australia, students may be suspended for ten consecutive days for a "serious breach" of school discipline;[64] Queensland permits suspensions of twenty days for behavior that is so serious that longer suspensions are warranted.[65] Indefinite suspensions or "rolling suspensions" are generally not permitted.

The authority to suspend or expel students from school also varies across jurisdictions. In Victoria[66] principals may suspend or expel students based on an order from the Minister. In South Australia[67] and Queensland,[68] principals are empowered to suspend or expel students. In Tasmania[69] the Secretary of Education, on the recommendation of principals, may suspend or expel students. In New South Wales,[70] the Director General has authority to suspend a student and the Minister may expel a student.

In Western Australia, principals may suspend students and may make a recommendation to the Chief Executive Officer (Director General) to exclude individuals.[71] In the ACT,[72] the Chief Executive Officer may suspend or expel students on the recommendations of principals. In the Northern Territory[73] principals are empowered to suspend students for up to one month while the Minister may make expulsions. Student who are expelled are generally not permitted to enroll at other schools without the consent of the Minister or a relevant authority.[74]

The temporary or permanent removal of students is considered a very serious matter and a serious disciplinary measure because it withdraws the right of students to attend school. Therefore, suspensions, exclusions, and expulsions are applied for more serious and persistent breaches of school rules and serious acts of misconduct.

The purpose of suspending or excluding students temporarily is primarily intended to ensure that the student's behavior can be appropriately managed and to maintain a safe school environment free of disruption and interference of daily school activities. It is not intended to be a punitive punishment but rather a measure to take positive action to remedy a student's behavior, provide a safe learning environment, and put in place appropriate support measures for the students and teachers.

By way of illustration the Tasmanian Department of Education states that suspension is aimed at ensuring students and parents are aware of the seriousness of the misconduct and to provide a process involving students and parents in managing the behavior and planning reentries to school.[75]

Students may be suspended, excluded, or expelled where principals, or relevant authorities, believe there are "reasonable grounds" for removing them temporarily or permanently from the school. Common grounds across all jurisdictions on which students may be suspended, excluded, or expelled include where individuals have:

- acted in manners threatening the safety or well-being of peers, members of staff, or other persons
- threatened to or perpetrated violence
- engaged in bullying behavior
- persistently refused to follow their school codes of conduct
- acted illegally
- interfered with the rights of others to learn
- behaved in a way threatening the good order of school activities
- caused, or are likely to cause, damage to property
- interfered with teachers' abilities to carry out their teaching
- failed to comply with reasonable instructions
- engaged in immoral conduct
- committed acts of violence or caused damage or destruction to property
- been in possession of a dangerous weapon at school
- been in possession of, used, or sold illegal drugs or prohibited substances[76]

Procedural Matters Relating to Suspension, Exclusion, and Expulsion

The procedures for dealing with suspensions, exclusions, and expulsions are found in legislation or education regulation and departmental guidelines.[77] These procedures in general aim to ensure that students, parents, and teachers are provided opportunities and time to assess and manage the behavior and to allow for the necessary support to be organized for children to return to school or, in cases of expulsions, to make other suitable arrangements for individuals to continue their education.

The fundamental principle of natural justice, which is essentially the right to be heard, and the right to a fair and impartial decision, underpins these procedures. The detail and clarity of procedures vary from one jurisdiction to another but, whether suspensions or expulsions, the procedural principles are mostly the same. For the purposes of this section, only the key aspects of procedural matters common to most jurisdictions are summarized below in terms of notice, hearings, and appeals.

Notice

An important aspect of procedural fairness is to ensure that the parties concerned receive proper notification. Proper notification helps to ensure that students and parents are informed about the appropriateness and fairness of decisions taken as well as to provide opportunities for students and parents to respond to the allegations and the actions taken by school officials. Therefore, provisions are made for students or their parents[78] to be consulted and notified in writing of proposed suspensions, exclusion, or expulsions, prior to the action coming into effect.[79] In addition to the notification of suspension, parents are provided with the school's guidelines and procedures on suspension or expulsion.

A Tasmanian guideline on suspension notes that oral communications, even if face to face, are insufficient for notification.[80] In cases where parents are separated or divorced, notification is generally provided to both parents, especially where they are both involved in the education of their children. The Northern Territory legislation specially refers to notification being given to the person who has "actual custody of the child."[81]

The content and details required for notices may vary between jurisdictions but they are mostly required to include specific details on the nature of the offenses, dates, and duration of exclusions, the responsibilities of the parties during the period of exclusion, support services that may be accessed, and information about appeals.[82]

Hearings

Procedural fairness includes the right to a fair hearing, that is, for affected students to "be given a reasonable opportunity to be heard" and an "opportunity to state their case."[83] Failure to provide for a fair hearing is usually a basis for a review of a decision. Hearings should be conducted within a reasonable time and not be unduly delayed. Prior to suspensions or expulsions, principals are generally required to convene meetings or disciplinary interviews with students concerned to consider whether to suspend them or to recommend that they be expelled. [84]

During interviews, students are given information about the allegations and an opportunity to respond. [85] Further, students are entitled to a suitable support person accompanying them at interviews, usually a parent but may be a peer or a teacher. It is also generally advisable that parents attend meetings involving young children and students with disabilities. [86]

If decisions are made to suspend students, their parents are notified in writing as discussed earlier. School officials generally require parents, along with other support staff, to attend meetings or parent conferences or resolution meetings to address the disciplinary matters and devise a structured plan for the students' return to school. The meetings usually consider reports from school counselors and other relevant support services. In Western Australia, School Advisory Discipline Panels consisting of at least three people may be established to advise the Minister on matters relating to student exclusions from school. At least one member of the panel must be a parent other than that of children to be excluded or community representative. [87]

Parents are responsible for their children during the periods of suspensions or exclusions. Most jurisdictions require principals to take reasonable steps to ensure that students have work to complete while they are not attending school. [88] Principals, in collaboration with students and their parents, must develop plans of work to be done by the children during their suspensions.

In some jurisdictions, students commit offenses if they fail to comply with written directions to undertake education or work during the periods of exclusion. South Australia is an example of where students may receive a penalty of A$200 for noncompliance. [89]

Principals in Queensland may impose a "behavior management condition" that requires students to participate in a "behavior management program." Such programs are conducted by appropriately qualified persons and are designed to help students not to reengage in the challenging behaviors. Behavior improvement conditions may be imposed if principals are reasonably satisfied that students enrolled at government schools have engaged in "challenging behavior," which is the basis for their exclusions from school. [90] Challenging behaviors relate to disobedience, misconduct, and other conduct by students that is prejudicial to the good order and management of their schools.

Appeals

Whether students have a right to appeal varies between states and territories. In general there is no right of appeal when students are suspended. In

Queensland students who are suspended for more than five days may make submissions to appeal suspensions. Students or their parent may appeal actions to expel on the basis that correct procedures have not been followed or an unfair decision has been made.[91] In Western Australia, there are only appeals based on process.[92]

Duty of Care and Student Misconduct

It is a well-established principle at common law that school authorities have a duty of care to students to provide safe school environments, and to protect students from harm caused by the negligence of others.[93] A "duty of care arises whenever a teacher/student relationship exists."[94]

In brief, a common law "duty of care" means that a principal or teacher has a duty to take reasonable care to protect a student from foreseeable harm or risk.[95] Under the law, a school is to "take such measures as are reasonable in the circumstances to protect a student under a teacher's care from risk of harm that the teacher should have reasonably foreseen. This approach requires not only protection from known hazards, but also protection from those that could reasonably arise and against which preventable measures could have been taken."[96] Therefore, for school authorities or teachers to be liable under common law, plaintiffs must prove that defendants owed a duty of care; officials or teachers fell below the required standard of care; the breach of duty of care caused the injury to the student; and the student's injury is compensable at law.[97]

In addition to the common law, Australian jurisdictions have civil liability legislation that codifies common law principles of negligence and is intended to "exist in the context of the tort of negligence and the common law of negligence that has developed over time."[98] As at common law, civil liability defines negligence as the "failure to exercise reasonable care and skill."[99]

Duty of Care

A school's duty of care falls within a recognized category at common law and has been considered in much litigation.[100] The law recognizes that there is a duty to protect children of immature age against the negligent conduct of others, or indeed of themselves, which may cause harm or injury.[101] This is coupled with the fact that, during school hours, children are beyond the control and protection of their parents and are placed under the control of school principals and teachers who are in the position to exercise authority over them while affording them, in the exercise of reasonable care, protection from injury.

Breach of Duty

As noted previously, the duty of care owed by schools to students is well established. As such, the main issue is whether school authorities or teachers breached their duty of care. School officials are not expected to protect students against all risks. Rather, they must take reasonable steps to ensure students are protected against foreseeable risks.[102] A breach of duty is likely to arise if school officials failed to take reasonable care in situations where the risk of injury or harm was foreseeable.[103]

At common law, the principle applied to determine the standard of care required is of a reasonable, prudent person ("the reasonable person test"), which may vary depending on the circumstances.[104] However, in the school context the courts have agreed that a higher standard of care is required for young children or children with disabilities. In *Australian Capital Territory Schools Authority v El Sheik*,[105] the court noted that the school authority was not liable for the injuries sustained by a fifteen-year-old student in a play fight because the teacher provided the standard of care of an ordinary reasonable teacher.

In *Victoria v. Bryar*[106] however a teacher was found to have breached her duty of care for failing to stop a fight involving firing pellets with elastic bands. The teacher knew that a fight was in progress and that it posed a significant danger. Still, the courts recognize that it is not always safe to intervene in fights. This is demonstrated in *Moran v. Victorian Institute of Teaching*[107] in which the Victorian Civil and Administrative Tribunal (VCAT) overturned the order of the Victorian Institute of Teaching to deregister a teacher because he failed to intervene in a schoolyard fight. The VCAT observed that it was reasonable for the teacher not to intervene in the fight if his physical safety was under threat.

The civil liability legislation has in large part followed the common law. Where a case of negligence is to be decided under civil liability legislation, three elements must be considered. The plaintiff must identify, and articulate clearly, the "risk of harm" in respect of which, it is alleged the defendant was obliged to take precautions.[108] Civil liability legislation provides that a person is *not* liable for harm or injury unless:[109] the risk was foreseeable; that is, it is a risk of which the person knew or ought to have known; the risk was "not insignificant"; and in the circumstances, a reasonable person in the person's position would have taken those precautions against risk of harm.

First, there is no liability unless the risk was foreseeable. Foreseeability is described in the civil liability legislation differently from the traditional common law description of something which "is not far-fetched or fanciful."[110] For a risk of harm to be deemed one that is foreseeable in accordance with the statute, plaintiffs must establish either actual knowledge in the defendants of the risk of harm, or else constructive knowledge; that is, the defendants ought to have known of the risk of harm.[111]

The second element is to determine whether the alleged risk of harm was "not insignificant."[112] The phrase "not insignificant" is intended to indicate a risk of a higher probability than is suggested by the phrase "not far-fetched and fanciful," but not so high as might be indicated by a phrase such as "a substantial risk." The word "significant" is apt to relate to a higher degree of probability.[113]

The third element, which closely reflects the common law, requires an analysis of the conduct of a reasonable person, in all of the circumstances of a case. In evaluating whether a reasonable person would have taken precautions against a risk of harm, the following factors are considered: the probability that the harm would occur if care were not taken; the likely seriousness of the harm; the burden of taking precautions to avoid the risk of harm; and the social utility of the activity that creates the risk of harm.

Causation

Where it has been established that school authorities or teachers have a duty of care, the duty has been breached, and students have been injured, it is necessary to address whether the breach of duty caused the injury.[114] In this situation, the onus is on the plaintiff to show causation. Civil liability legislation requires that the negligence caused the particular harm which is determined by factual causation, and scope of liability.[115]

A finding that negligence caused a particular harm therefore comprises the following elements: (a) that the negligence was a necessary condition of the occurrence of the harm ("factual causation"), and (b) that it is appropriate for the scope of the negligent person's liability to extend to the harm so caused ("scope of liability").[116]

The duty of care in relation to student misconduct is illustrated in *"H" v State of New South Wales*[117] in which a secondary school student ("H") was assaulted and stabbed by a fellow student ("G") on the school playground. The injured student brought an action in tort claiming that school authorities breached their duty of care and were liable for the physical and psychological injuries he suffered when threatened and stabbed by G.

The court held that school authorities were negligent because there were material breaches of the duty of care that they owed to the student. It was held that two teachers failed in their obligations toward the student following his initial confrontation with G who subsequently assaulted and stabbed him while the students were lining up to enter a classroom. The court noted that despite the gravity of the first confrontation, no steps had been taken by the teachers to intervene and counsel the students to ensure that the matter was resolved.[118]

The court ruled that the risk of the student being harmed by G was reasonably foreseeable and likely to occur, but no effort was made to ensure his safety. It was held that the risk of injury "was not insignificant."[119] It was contended that had the student been appropriately isolated in accordance with the school policy at the time while he remained at school following the death threat or taken home, he would not have been attacked and stabbed. The failure to take reasonable steps to protect the student from harm resulted in injuries. Damages awarded to the plaintiff amounted to A$627,468, including loss of earning capacity.[120]

CONCLUSION

Australian education authorities, as in any other country, face the ongoing challenge of managing student behavior and misconduct no matter how trivial or serious. A fundamental role of principals and teachers is to develop policies and practices based on the relevant legislation and regulations that are ultimately aimed at promoting positive behavior and ensuring that students can achieve their full potential in an environment that is safe, secure, and supportive.

Principals and teachers have statutory and common law authority to discipline students and maintain orderly environments. This authority is found in relevant state legislation and regulations, which provide the legal basis for developing and implementing school behavior management plans. Australia's nine jurisdictions have education laws, regulations, and guidelines that are sometimes similar and sometimes different, a result which leads to a varied response to the matter of student misconduct. Even so, there are common principles and approaches spanning all jurisdictions.

Some aspects of student misconduct are explicitly covered in the legislation while others are implied or absent altogether. There are commendable initiatives to put in place the necessary best practice by way of policies and approaches for responding to and reducing student misconduct.

School authorities have an ongoing duty to regularly review and monitor the effectiveness and efficiency of school discipline policies and practices with a view to making continuous improvement in managing student behavior while reducing misconduct in schools, and creating safe, orderly schools.

KEY POINTS

1. Each Australian jurisdiction is responsible for creating safe and orderly school environments and for regulating student behavior in schools. However, the National Safe Schools Framework provides for a more coherent and consistent approach to managing school discipline.

2. All schools in Australia are required to have a school behavior management policy in place, which also deals with school bullying either as an integrated or separate policy. Policies must be well documented and communicated to the school community.

3. In all Australian jurisdictions the fundamental principles of equity, dignity, nondiscrimination, and natural justice underpin the management of school discipline.

4. Although schools have at their disposal a wide range of strategies for managing school discipline, strategies that deal with more serious offenses such as suspension and expulsion, corporal punishments and time-out are contained in relevant education legislation and regulations, which may vary between Australian states and territories.

5. Schools have a duty of care at common law and statutory law to take reasonable steps to ensure the safety and security of all students.

NOTES

1. The *Commonwealth of Australia Constitution Act* [9 July 1900] http://www.comlaw.gov.au/Details/C2013Q00005.

2. *Northern Territory (Self-Governing) Act 1978* (Cth) and *Australian Capital Territory (Self-Governing) Act 1988* (Cth).

3. John Carvan, *Understanding the Australian Legal System*, 6th ed. (LawBook Co, 2009).

4. Section 122 of the Australian Constitution empowers the Commonwealth Parliament to make laws in relation to the territories. The self-governing territories have limited lawmaking powers that the Commonwealth may revoke.

5. Section 51 of the Australian Constitution lists forty heads of power, including the addition of § 51xxiiiA, in terms of which the Commonwealth can legislate for the "peace, order and good government of the Commonwealth." There is no specific head of power for education. Commonwealth laws on education are therefore based on other heads of powers, notably the corporations power and trade and commerce power.

6. Where there is a conflict of laws, section 109 of the Constitution states that a valid Commonwealth law prevails over an inconsistent valid state law to the extent of the inconsistency.

7. Andy Gibson and Douglas Fraser, *Business Law* (Pearson, 2013).

8. See, for example, *Constitution Act 1889* (WA), §5 and *Constitution Act 1902* (NSW) §5.

9. The Commonwealth government is responsible for funding higher education. This chapter covers primary and secondary schooling only. Higher education, early childhood education, adult education, and vocational training are not included.

10. The term "private school" is used to include independent schools and Catholic schools. The majority of nongovernment schools have some religious affiliation and some two-thirds of nongovernment school students are enrolled in Catholic schools: Independent Schools Council of Australia (ISCA) http://www.isca.edu.au/, 3 May 2014.

11. *Education Act 2004* (ACT) Chapter 4; *Education Act 1990* (NSW) Part 7; *Education Act* (NT) Part 7; *Education Act 1994* (Tas) Part 5; *School Education Act 1999* (WA) Part 4.

12. In Western Australia the school leaving age is seventeen: *School Education Act 1999* (WA) § 6. For a summary of school data, see the Australian Curriculum, Assessment and Reporting Authority, The National Report on Schooling 2011, http://www.acara.edu.au/reporting/national_report_on_schooling_2011/national_report_on_schooling_2_1.html.

13. *Education Act 2004* (ACT) § 20; *Education Act 1990* (NSW) § 19, § 35; *Education Act 2007* (NT) § 6, § 8; *Education (General Provisions) Act 2006* (Qld) § 12, § 13; *Education Act 1972* (SA) § 6, § 7, § 9, § 12; *Education Act 1994* (Tas) § 18; *Education and Training Reform Act 2006* (Vic) Chapter 5, Part 5.2; *School Education Act 1999* (WA) § 61, § 214, § 215, § 216.

14. Ibid.

15. *School Education Act 1999* (WA) § 63; *Education Act 2004* (ACT) § 21.

16. See, for example, Government of Queensland, Department of Education, Training and Employment, *Responsible Behaviour Plan for Students*, http://education.qld.gov.au/studentservices/behaviour/bm-plans.html.

17. *School Education Act 1999* (WA) § 63(1).

18. *School Education Regulations 2000* (WA) reg 69. See also *Education (General Provision) Regulation 2006* (Qld), reg 5; *Education Regulations 2012* (SA) reg 42.

19. *Education Act 2004* (ACT) § 38; *Education Act 1990* (NSW) § 36; *Education Act* (NT) § 71; *Education (General Provisions) Act 2006* (Qld) § 79; *Education Act 1972* (SA) § 85; *Education Act 1994* (Tas) § 26; *Education and Training Reform Act 2006* (Vic) § 2.3.5; *School Education Act 1999* (WA) § 128.

20. *School Education Act 1999* (WA) § 125 unless the Minister exempts a school from having a council.

21. *Education Act 1972* (SA) § 83(1).

22. *Education Act 2004* (ACT) § 38.

23. *School Education Act 1999* (WA) § 130. An incorporated school council may obtain funds for the school but may not borrow money.

24. Additional functions are to take part in the selection of, but not the appointment of, the school principal or any other member of the teaching staff and to carry out any other function prescribed by the regulations for the purposes of section 129.

25. *Education Act 1994* (Tas) § 26.

26. *Education Act 2007* (NT) § 71. School councils are incorporated as legal entities with perpetual succession.

27. *Education Act 1990* (NSW) § 36.

28. *Education (General Provisions) Act 2006* (Qld) § 79.

29. *Education Act 2004* (ACT) § 39, § 46; *Education Act 1990* (NSW) § 36; *Education Act* (NT) § 71C, § 71D; *Education (General Provisions) Act 2006* (Qld) § 81; *Education Act 1972* (SA) § 83; *Education Act 1994* (Tas) § 27; *Education and Training Reform Act 2006* (Vic) § 2.3.5; *School Education Act 1999* (WA) § 128, § 133.

30. These guiding principles are generally reflected in education legislation and policies. See, for example, *Education Act 2004* (ACT) § 7; *Education Act 1990* (NSW) § 4; *Education (General Provisions) Act 2006* (Qld) § 7; *Education and Training Reform Act 2006* (Vic) § 1.2.1.

31. Government of Queensland, Department of Education, Training and Employment, *The Code of School Behaviour*, http://education.qld.gov.au/publication/production/reports/pdfs/code-school-behaviour-a4.pdf.

32. Government of Tasmania, Department of Education, *Discipline Guidelines* https://www.education.tas.gov.au/documentcentre/Documents/Discipline-Guidelines.pdf, p. 3 May 2014.

33. New South Wales Department of Education and Communities, *Student Discipline in Government Schools Policy* https://www.det.nsw.edu.au/policies/student_serv/discipline/stu_discip_gov/PD20060316.shtml.

34. Student Learning and Support Services Taskforce of the Ministerial Council on Education, Employment, Training and Youth Affairs. *National Safe Schools Framework* http://www.education.gov.au/national-safe-schools-framework-0.

35. Australian Government, Department of Education, *The National Safe Schools Framework* (Revised 2010; Updated 2013), http://safeschoolshub.edu.au/.

36. Ibid. 2.

37. Ibid. 5.

38. All schools are expected to have anti-bullying policies. The NSSF provides that schools have clearly communicated procedures for staff to follow when responding to incidents of

student harm from child maltreatment, harassment, aggression, violence, bullying, or misuse of technology.

39. *Education Act 2004* (ACT) § 36; *Education Act 1990* (NSW) § 35; *Education (General Provisions) Act 2006* (Qld) § 275; *Education Act 1994* (Tas) § 38; *Education and Training Reform Act 2006* (Vic) § 2.2.19; *School Education Act 1999* (WA) § 88.

40. Jane Edwards, Andrew Knott, and Dan Riley, *Australian Schools and the Law* (LBC Information Services, 1997), 19.

41. *Education Act 1990* (NWS) § 35(2)(A), § 47(h).

42. *Education Act 1994* (Tas) § 82A.

43. *Education and Training Reform Act 2006* (Vic) § 2.4.60(1)(f), § 4.3.1(6)(a).

44. *Education Act 2004* (ACT) § 7(4).

45. *School Education Regulations 2000* (WA) § 40(2).

46. *Criminal Code 1899* (Qld), § 280 (Domestic Discipline).

47. Government of Queensland, Department of Education, Training and Employment, *The Code of School Behaviour*, http://education.qld.gov.au/publication/production/reports/pdfs/code-school-behaviour-a4.pdf.

48. *Education Act 1990* (NSW) § 3.

49. *Education and Training Reform Regulations 2007* (Vic) reg 15. See also *School Education Regulations 2000* (WA) reg 38.

50. *Education Act 1990* (NSW) § 2B.

51. See, for example, *Education (General Provisions) Act 2006* (Qld) § 276; Tasmania Government, Department of Education, *Discipline Guidelines: Detention*, http://www.education.tas.gov.au/dept/legislation/discipline/detention; Government of Victoria, Department of Education and Early Childhood Development, Student Engagement and Inclusion Guidance 2014, Disciplinary Measures, http://www.education.vic.gov.au/school/principals/participation/Pages/studentengagementguidance.aspx.

52. *Education Act 1994* (Tas) § 37(b).

53. Ibid.

54. Tasmania Government, Department of Education, *Discipline Guidelines: Detention*, http://www.education.tas.gov.au/dept/legislation/discipline/detention.

55. *Education Regulations 2012* (SA) reg 43(3).

56. *School Education Regulations 2000* (WA) regs 40–42.

57. Tasmania Government, Department of Education, Discipline Guidelines: Detention, http://www.education.tas.gov.au/dept/legislation/discipline/detention.

58. See, for example, Government of New South Wales, Department of Education and Communities, Guidelines for the Use of Time-out Strategies Including Dedicated Time-out Rooms (2011) https://www.det.nsw.edu.au/policies/student_serv/discipline/stu_discip_gov/timeout_gui.pdf; Queensland, Safe, Supportive Discipline School Environment http://ppr.det.qld.gov.au/education/learning/Pages/Safe,-Supportive-and-Disciplined-School-Environment.aspx; Tasmania Government, Department of Education, Discipline Guidelines: Time-out http://www.education.tas.gov.au/dept/legislation/discipline/detention.

59. Ibid.

60. Ibid.

61. Government of New South Wales, Department of Education and Communities, *Guidelines for the Use of Time-out Strategies Including Dedicated Time-out Rooms* (2011) https://www.det.nsw.edu.au/policies/student_serv/discipline/stu_discip_gov/timeout_gui.pdf.

62. Ibid. 2.

63. Not all jurisdictions expressly distinguish between suspension and exclusion; however, exclusion is generally for a period exceeding two weeks (ten schools days). See, for example, *Education Regulation 2012* (SA) regs 44, 45 and *Education Act 1994* (Tas) § 38(1).

64. *School Education Regulations 2000* (WA) reg 43(1)(b).

65. *Education (General Provisions) Act 2006* (Qld) § 285(2)(b).

66. *Education and Training Reform Act 2006* (Vic) § 2.2.19.

67. *Education Regulations 2012* (SA) regs 43–45. In South Australia the *Education Act* does not include provisions relating to student suspension and expulsion.

68. *Education (General Provisions) Act 2006* (Qld) § 285(2).

69. *Education Act 1994* (Tas) § 38.

70. *Education Act 1990* (NSW) § 35(3).

71. *School Education Act 1999* (WA) § 90, § 92.

72. *Education Act 2004* (ACT) § 36.

73. *Education Act 2007* (NT) § 27, § 28.

74. *Education Act 1990* (NSW) § 35(5); *Education Act 2007* (NT) § 29A; *Education Regulations 2012* (SA) reg 45.

75. Tasmania Government, Department of Education, *Discipline Guidelines: Suspension* http://www.education.tas.gov.au/dept/legislation/discipline/suspension-expulsion.

76. See eg, *Education (General Provisions) Act* (Qld), § 284, 288B; *Education Regulations 2012* (SA), regs 48; *Education Act 1994* (Tas) § 37; *School Education Act 1999* (WA) § 91. *Education Act 2002* (ACT) § 38(1); *Education Act 2007* (NT) § 27(1).

77. In South Australia the provisions for suspension and expulsions are found in the *Education Regulations 2012* (SA).

78. A parent includes the person (guardian, caregiver) who has custody or care of the child. In the case of children in a care-home then the case manager should be present.

79. *Education Act 2004* (ACT) § 36(4)(a)–(5)(a); *Education Act* (NT) § 21(2); *Education (General Provisions) Act 2006* (Qld) § 283(2)–(3). NSW Suspension and Expulsion Procedures, above n 112, 7.1.2, 7.2.1, 7.2.2.

80. Tasmania Government, Department of Education, *Discipline Guidelines: Suspension*, http://www.education.tas.gov.au/dept/legislation/discipline/suspension-expulsion.

81. *Education Act* (NT) § 27(3), § 28(3).

82. *Education (General Provisions) Act 2006* (Qld) § 288C; *Education Act 2004* (ACT) § 36.

83. Australian Capital Territory, Education and Training Directorate, and Training Suspension, Exclusion or Transfer of Students in ACT Public Schools (Transitional Policy) 2010. Attachment B sets out a comprehensive explanation of procedural fairness and natural justice.

84. *Education Act 2004* (ACT) § 36(4)(b) and (5)(b); NSW Suspension and Expulsion Procedures, above n 112, 6.3.5.

85. *Education Act 2004* (ACT) § 36(5)(c);

86. *Education and Training Reform Act 2006* (Vic) § 2.2.19; *Education (General Provisions) Act 2006* (Qld) § 278.

87. *School Education Act 1999* (WA) § 93.

88. *Education Act 2004* (ACT) § 36(5)(d); *Education (General Provisions) Act 2006* (Qld) § 284, § 294; *School Education Regulations 2000* (WA) reg 46.

89. *Education Regulations 2012* (SA) reg 45(5).

90. *Education (General Provisions) Act 2006* (Qld) § 323, § 324.

91. *Education and Training Reform Act 2006* (Vic) § 2.2.19; *School Education Act 1999* (WA) § 96; *Education Act 1994* (Tas) § 38(4); *Education (General Provisions) Act 2006* (Qld) § 287; *Education Regulations 2012* (SA) reg 50.

92. *School Education Act 1999* (WA) § 96(2).

93. See eg, *Geyer v. Downs* (1977) 138 CLR 911 and *Commonwealth v. Introvigne* (1982) 150 CLR 258.

94. *"H" v. State of New South Wales* [2009] NSWDC 193 [106].

95. Jim Jackson and Sally Varnham, *Law for Educators* (LexisNexis Butterworths, 2007).

96. *"H" v. State of New South Wales* [2009] NSWDC 193, 106.

97. Ibid.

98. *Garzo v. Liverpool/Campbelltown Christian School Limited* [2011] NSWSC 292, [54].

99. *Civil Liability Act 2002* (NSW) § 5. Cf with the *Civil Liability Act 2003* (Qld) that defines "duty of care" as "a duty to take reasonable care or to exercise reasonable skill" (Schedule 2).

100. See, for example, *Ramsay v. Larsen* [1964] HCA 40; *Richard's v. State of Victoria* (1969) VR 136, 138–39; *Australian Capital Territory Schools Authority v. El Sheik* [2000] FCA 931; *Trustees of the Roman Catholic Church for the Diocese of Canberra and Goulburn v. Hadba* [2005] HCA 31 (15 June 2005); *New South Wales v. Lepore, Samin v. Queensland, Rich v. Queensland* [2003] HCA 4 (6 February).

101. See n 93.

102. *Ramsay v. Larsen* [1964] HCA 40 (29 July 1964); *Richards v. State of Victoria* (1969) VR 136; *Kondis v. State Transport Authority* (1984) 152 CLR 672; *The Trustees of the Roman Catholic Church for the Archdiocese of Sydney v. Kondrajian* [2001] NSWCA 308.

103. Ibid.

104. Carolyn Sappideen and Prue Vines, *Fleming's The Law of Torts*, 10th ed. (Thomson Reuters, 2011); Frances McGlone and Amanda Stickley, *Australian Torts Law*, 2nd ed. (Lexis-Nexis Butterworths, 2009).

105. *Australian Capital Territory Schools Authority v. El Sheik* [2000] FCA 931.

106. *Victoria v. Bryar* (1970) 44 ALJR 1745.

107. *Moran v. Victorian Institute of Teaching* [2007] VCAT 1311 (31 July 2007)

108. *Garzo v. Liverpool/Campbelltown Christian School Limited* [2011] NSWSC 292, [67].

109. *Civil Law (Wrongs) Act 2002* (ACT) § 43; *Civil Liability Act 2002* (NSW) § 5B; *Civil Liability Act 2003* (Qld) § 9; *Civil Liability Act 1936* (SA) § 32; *Civil Liability Act 2002* (Tas) § 11; *Wrongs Act 1958* (Vic) § 48; *Civil Liability Act 2002* (WA) § 5B.

110. *Garzo v. Liverpool/Campbelltown Christian School Limited* [2011] NSWSC 292, [67].

111. *Garzo v. Liverpool/Campbelltown Christian School Limited* [2011] NSWSC 292, [68].

112. *Garzo v. Liverpool/Campbelltown Christian School Limited* [2011] NSWSC 292, [101], [102]. The phrase derives from the final report of the Review of the Law of Negligence (the Ipp Report) that was published in September 2002.

113. Ibid.

114. *"H" v. State of New South Wales* [2009] NSWDC 193.

115. *Garzo v. Liverpool/Campbelltown Christian School Limited* [2011] NSWSC 292, 255. See also, civil liability legislation above n 126, ACT § 45; NSW § 5D; Old § 11; SA § 34; Tas § 13; Vic § 51; WA § 5C.

116. *Civil Law (Wrongs) Act 2002* (ACT) § 45; *Civil Liability Act 2002* (NSW) § 5D; *Civil Liability Act 2003* (Qld) § 11; *Civil Liability Act 1936* (SA) § 34; *Civil Liability Act 2002* (Tas) § 1; *Wrongs Act 1958* (Vic) § 51; *Civil Liability Act 2002* (WA) § 5C.

117. *"H" v. State of New South Wales* [2009] NSWDC 193.

118. Ibid [7], [147].

119. Ibid [150], [155].

120. Ibid [164], [542].

Chapter Two

Student Misconduct and School Responses in Aotearoa New Zealand

Safety and Sensibility

Sally Varnham

New Zealand, a constitutional monarchy which sits in the South Pacific Ocean to the southeast of Australia, has a population of four and a half million of which 15 percent are indigenous Maori people. As originally a colony and then a Dominion of the British Empire, New Zealand's political system is based on a Westminster democracy and its legal system is a combination of legislation and common law.

Prior to 1989 the executive arm of government was based largely on public ownership. The Labour Administration, elected in 1987, embarked on a program of reducing the state bureaucracy and increasing corporatization and privatization of the public service. The education system was a large part of the changes and the basis on which state education was provided underwent massive reform. This was known as "Tomorrow's Schools: The Reform of Education Administration in New Zealand" and legislated for primarily in the Education Act 1989; although parts of the original Education Act 1964 remain, there have been subsequent amendments.

The reforms relating to the provision of education in New Zealand were underpinned by the dual philosophies of community empowerment and individual choice. The administration of all state schools was devolved from central government to a system where each school is administered by a locally elected Board of Trustees. This board consists of parents, students, and representatives from teaching staffs and school principals.

Each board receives public funding although teacher salaries are still paid centrally.

While the Department of Education was disestablished, there remains the Ministry of Education which has a policy function.

State education is provided pursuant to the Education Acts 1964 and 1989 and its amendments, and is free and compulsory between the ages of six and sixteen years.[1] Within the compulsory education system in the primary (years one to seven) and secondary (years eight to twelve) there are primarily three types of schools: state, integrated, and private.

Within state education there are schools designated as *Kura Kaupapa Maori* in which *Te Reo Maori* (the Maori language) is the principal language of instruction. These schools are required by the charters to operate in accordance with *Te Aho Matua*, a statement setting out a particular approach to teaching and learning.[2] The largest proportion of children in New Zealand is educated in the state sector for both primary and secondary years; state schools are zoned with their catchment in particular areas.

State integrated schools are those which were previously private schools but which elected, under the Private Schools Conditional Integration Act 1975, to become part of the state system while retaining their "special character." The majority of denominational schools in New Zealand are state integrated. Schools which remain private are independent but must be registered and are subject to regular inspections under the Education Act 1989.[3]

It is possible for parents to educate their children at home but to do so require exemptions from compulsory enrollment and attendance at a school.[4] Evidence shows that the numbers of children being homeschooled is decreasing in relation to the numbers of school aged children: in 2001, 5,689 children were homeschooled and in 2013 there were 5,521.[5]

Home educators are subject to regular inspections as required by the Secretary for Education.[6] Although there are many reasons given for a parent's decision to home educate, anecdotal evidence suggests that in some instances parents choose this alternative for children who are suspended from formal schooling because of behavioral difficulties.

Schools are managed by boards and principals. Boards have, subject to the laws of New Zealand, complete discretion to control the management of their schools as they "think fit"; school principals are vested as a board's chief executive in relation to control and management.

All government, integrated, and private schools in New Zealand must teach the National Curriculum and are subject to regular review by the Chief Officer of the Education Review Office.[7] Section 3 of the Education Act 1989 provides that all children have a right to education while section 8 states that those with special educational needs have the same rights to enroll and receive education in state schools as people who do not.

Since the inception of a policy known as Special Education 2000, children with special needs are "mainstreamed" within regular schools in the state education system with resources provided to those schools on an individual child demonstrated need basis. The policy of mainstreaming is important within the context of school safety, student behavior, and school discipline, particularly in light of the problems faced by schools when children with disabilities exhibit behaviors which pose risks to others. In comparative jurisdictions, school authorities have been faced with discrimination actions in such circumstances, for example, in Australia, *Purvis on behalf of Daniel Hoggan v. State of New South Wales (Department of Education and Training)*,[8] dealt with just this issue.

Discrimination in the context of discipline of children with disabilities was raised recently in the High Court of New Zealand in *"A" v. Hutchinson and The Board of Trustees of Green Bay High School.*[9] However, the discrimination issue was not further argued and the matter proceeded successfully on the basis of Judicial Review.[10] This course of action is in common with the UK case of *Re L (a minor by his father and litigation friend)*[11] although in that instance the court did not agree that the school's decision should be overturned.

In New Zealand antidiscrimination litigation challenging stand-downs, suspension, exclusion, or expulsion is negligible. Even so, the Human Rights Disability Commissioner has noted a considerable number of complaints of discrimination made to the commission under the Human Rights Act 1993.[12]

In a 2014 statement of support for the successful Judicial Review and reinstatement of the student back into school by the New Zealand High Court in "A," discussed next, the Commissioner is quoted as saying: "Regrettably, the Human Rights Commission continues to receive large numbers of complaints each year about disabled students being disadvantaged because of inadequate recognition of their support needs."[13]

All teachers in New Zealand must be registered with the Teachers Council which is the professional and regulatory body for teachers working in English and Māori medium settings in the compulsory education sector. The Teachers Council is an autonomous Crown entity which has as its function the support and maintenance of professional teaching standards through competence and discipline bodies. The Teachers Council Code of Ethics places a legal obligation on registered teachers to "promote the physical, emotional, social, intellectual and spiritual wellbeing of learners."

STUDENT DISCIPLINE

Corporal punishment is forbidden in all New Zealand schools.[14] Principals and school boards of trustees have the power to exclude students from school in various ways under sections 13-18 of the Education Act 1989 and the Education (Stand-Down, Suspension, Exclusion and Expulsion) Rules 1999.

These instruments provide a range of responses in terms of school exclusions for misconduct—stand-downs, suspensions, exclusions, and expulsions.

Stand-downs were introduced in 1999 as the formal removal of children from schools for short periods of time. Children may be stood down for no more than five school days in one term and no more than ten school days in one year. Suspensions mean the formal removal of children from schools until boards of trustees decide the outcomes at suspension meetings.

Exclusions mean the formal removal of children from schools with the requirement that they be enrolled in alternative education, either at another school or to learn by correspondence classes. Expulsions mean the formal removal of children from schools and only may be imposed for those over sixteen.

Section 13 of the Education Act sets out the purpose of the different forms of school exclusions as:

1. To provide a range of responses to varying degrees of seriousness of misconduct,
2. To ensure that the disruption to the student's attendance is minimalized and their return to school is facilitated,
3. To ensure that each child is dealt with in accordance with principles of natural justice or due process.

This statement of purposes was inserted by section 7 of the Education Amendment Act (No 2) 1998 and, it has been argued, may "well be considered to enhance the prospects of a successful challenge to disciplinary action" if it could be shown that the Principal or Board of Trustees was motivated by some other less laudable concern. [15]

Section 14 provides that the grounds on which principals of state schools may stand-down or suspend children if they are "satisfied on reasonable grounds" that the student engaged in:

1. Gross misconduct or continual disobedience which is a harmful or dangerous example to other students at the school; or,
2. Because of the student's behavior, it is likely that that student, or other students at the school, will be seriously harmed if the student is not stood down or suspended.

Both of these grounds clearly prioritize the safety of the school community as the justification for any form of school exclusion. This includes the student engaging in the misconduct.

The stand-down is designed to be a "short sharp shock" to students and it is clearly anticipated that students will be assimilated back in to their school communities after having some time to reflect on their actions. It also allows for principals to remove a source of danger when needed to protect the school community without the need for lengthy procedures. The restrictions on stand-downs in terms of length and frequency are strictly limited to ensure such a procedure is not over-used in the case of an individual child.

If children are suspended by their principals, the matters must be referred to their school boards of trustees. Section 17B of the Education Act 1989 provides that students and their parents and representatives may attend and speak at the board meetings when their suspensions are being considered and they have a right to have their views considered.

Boards, after considering the matters with observance to principles of natural justice may, if children are under sixteen,[16] lift the suspensions unconditionally or, subject them to reasonable conditions; or extend the suspensions conditionally for reasonable periods. Where the seriousness of the behavior warrants longer exclusion responses, board may extend the suspensions and require students to be enrolled in other schools.

In relation to this latter provision, section 15 places a responsibility on school boards to ensure that the conditions imposed are aimed at facilitating students' returns to school. Section 15 (4) and (5) make provisions for the situations when a child fails to comply with the conditions or principals and are unable to arrange attendance at other schools, with the Secretary for Education having the final responsibility to ensure that those who are suspended have the ability to receive an education, either at another school or by correspondence. Section 17 sets out board powers when suspended children are over sixteen which are in a similar vein but without the responsibility to arrange alternative education. Principals may expel such children.[17]

These provisions place strong emphases also on the rights of children to an education.[18] These provisions aim to address the need to ensure safe educational environments for all children, while being cognizant and respectful of the right to education of children who engage in misconduct. Following suspensions or stand-downs, principals have the duty imposed under Section 17A that all reasonable steps are taken to ensure that children continue to receive educations and to minimize any educational disadvantage.

The Ministry of Education Guidelines provide good practice for boards of trustees and principals when making decisions relating "to the exclusion of children from school and to assist current practice in relation to serious behavioural incidents in your school, including serious misconduct and/or violent behaviour that may or may not result in stand-downs, suspensions, exclusion and expulsion."[19]

The guidelines specify that board suspensions meetings are automatic reviews of the decisions of principals to suspend students. The purpose of these meetings is to focus on "reviewing the principal's decision, hearing from everyone and finding the way forward."[20] However, it is not in the nature of a hearing.

At the same time, the guidelines indicate that exclusions should only be imposed in circumstances that justify the most serious response, and they direct the board to balance all the factors, such as whether the student's "gross misconduct" or behavior posed a serious risk of harm, the part played by the student's individual circumstances, how other students were affected.[21]

STUDENT MISCONDUCT

Statistics available from the Ministry of Education website from the 2012 year show that stand-downs from state and integrated schools decreased from 2.2 percent of the student population recorded in 2008, to 1.8 percent, and suspensions were down from 0.6 percent to 0.4 percent. Physical assaults on other students were the main reason for stand-downs while the main behaviors leading to suspension and exclusion were "continual disobedience," physical assault on other students, and drugs.[22]

In 2012, 0.1 percent of students were expelled, effectively ending their schooling. The main reason for this was substance abuse, including drugs, followed by physical assault on other students and continual disobedience.

School-related bullying is a universal problem and the high incidence occurring in New Zealand is a major concern. Studies have shown that physical and emotional bullying by peers is a common experience for the children who attend New Zealand schools.[23]

A study into school safety conducted in 2009 by the Office of the Children's Commissioner defined bullying as hitting, kicking, or use of force of any way; teasing, making rude gestures, name calling, or leaving a child out of things on purpose; physical, verbal (including text and cyber-bullying), and nonverbal (being left out).

To be defined as "bullying" those things had to have happened more than once and caused either physical or emotional hurt.[24] The decision to undertake the inquiry was made both following a number of incidents which received media publicity and due to concern at the ongoing complaints about bullying and violence to children's help and advice lines.[25]

The report refers to high levels of physical and emotional bullying while pointing to an international study which rates New Zealand schools among the worst in the world.[26] The study found that while most schools have clear policies and procedures to address the issue of bullying, educators in some schools choose not to acknowledge that bullying exists and therefore failed to address it effectively.

It was the researcher's view in the report that there is a lack of consistency in schools across New Zealand in how they deal with issues relating to school safety; the report made a large number of recommendations for facilitating change and creating safer schools. These changes are based largely on whole-school approaches to student behavior on a restorative rather than retributive basis, and these are discussed later in this chapter in the section "Behavior Management."

Concurrent to the previously discussed study and following receipt of a complaint from parents of students subjected to bullying in a secondary school, the Human Rights Commission (HRC) undertook an inquiry into bullying and violence in New Zealand schools. The HRC did so on the basis that such activity compromises a child's right to education and to personal security and as such is a human rights violation.

In its report, "School Violence, Bullying and Abuse: A Human Rights Analysis," the HRC offered a series of recommendations for inclusion in Ministry of Education Guidelines designed to provide support to schools in relation to stand-downs, suspensions, exclusions, and expulsions.[27]

THE RIGHT TO EDUCATION, SCHOOL SAFETY AND RESPONSIBILITY

The right to education is affirmed in Article 28(1) United Nations Convention on the Rights of the Child and is specifically legislated for in New Zealand in section 3 of the Education Act 1989. The regime of education policy and legislation places a strong responsibility on educators in respect of the maintenance of educational environments which are safe and conducive to all students having the best conditions to take advantage of educational opportunities.

School boards of trustees are bound by the National Administration Guidelines (NAGs) and National Education Guidelines (NEGs) which set out their responsibilities.[28] NAG 5 imposes a legal obligation on boards to provide safe physical and emotional environments for students.[29] Section 60A of the Education Act 1989 requires teachers/schools to report to parents matters that may put students at risk of not achieving (NAG 1).

Section 77 of the Education Act 1989 requires principals of state schools to take all reasonable steps to ensure that parents are informed of matters preventing or slowing student progress through school or harming students' relationships with teachers or peers. Arguably, this provision places a positive duty on principals to consider the pastoral care of all students within their care in the state system.

In terms of student misbehavior, it could be asserted that principals have a duty to consider many options in dealings with all parties, bullies, those manifesting violent and disruptive behavior, and victims. Viewed in terms of students whose behavior is threatening the safety of others, it means that principals must ensure as far as possible that they receive the help they need to change their behavior.

The second part of Section 77 contains a duty to ensure that parents are involved in dealing with behavioral problems.[30] Clearly a combination of these provisions requires educators to explore all restorative responses before resorting to exclusions. This, of course, must be balanced against the right of all students to safe educational environments and clearly, in terms of acute threats of violence, the duty of educators to ensure that the safety of the whole school community must be uppermost.[31]

School boards of trustees are bound by any legislation currently in force to ensure the safety of students and common law by which a duty of care is imposed on them.[32] In addition to education legislation, school administrators are also subject to a plethora of other instruments. Notably the Health and Safety in Employment Act 1992 provides for compliance with this act and with the Ministry of Education's Health and Safety Code of Practice for state and state integrated schools.[33]

Under these guidelines educators are obliged to take all practicable steps to prevent "hazards" from harming people; "hazards" include behavior with the potential to cause physical, emotional, or psychological harm. Educators who are not dealing effectively with bullying in all ways which are reasonably possible, could well face prosecution under this act.

Two international conventions, ratified by New Zealand, impact on the responsibilities of school authorities in terms of safety. Although the provisions of international conventions must be incorporated in domestic legislation in order to have the force of law, there is authority for the view that their ratification creates legitimate expectations that their principles will be adhered to.[34]

These two instruments are the United Nations Convention on the Rights of the Child which affirms a right to protection from all forms of violence (Article 19); a right to education that develops respect for children's human rights, identity, and democracy (Article 28); and a right for education to be delivered in a spirit of peace (Article 29). The International Covenant on Economic, Social and Cultural Rights requires education to demonstrate respect for human rights and fundamental freedoms; and education experiences should be offered in an environment that is consistent with human dignity.[35]

The founding document of New Zealand is the Treaty of Waitangi which was entered into in 1840 between Queen Victoria as representing the British Empire and the indigenous Maori peoples. The NAGs require schools to operate consistently with the principles of the treaty. This responsibility demands that education policy reflects the concept of "turangawaewae," or the right to belong.

The aim of the Ministry of Education to ensure that each Maori child has the best possible educational opportunity is contained in current Maori edu-

cation strategies.[36] The fact remains, though, that Maori children are disproportionately represented in the numbers of school suspensions.[37]

Multiple reasons are advanced for this going back fundamentally to the
imposition of a compulsory white Anglo-Saxon or "pakeha" education system on Maori from the passing of the first Education Act 1877. It has been
argued that from that time education was used by the New Zealand government "as a means of social control and assimilation."[38] It is further argued
that current policies:

> arrive out of the social history and culture of the dominant race. . . .These
> epistemologies logically reflect and reinforce that social history and the con-
> trolling position of that racial group (while excluding the epistemologies of
> other races/cultures), and this has negative results for people of colour in
> general.[39]

In an attempt to reduce the relatively high level of school exclusion and
disengagement of Maori children, the Ministry of Education has established
guidelines for boards of trustees and schools particularly aimed at engaging
with Maori parents, whanau, and communities.[40]

Despite numerous government education strategies, there remains in New
Zealand a significant economic discrepancy between Maori and Pakeha.
Moreover, it is clear that disengagement from education through school dis-
ciplinary measures plays a large part in this.[41]

It is argued that, not only does the education system not work for Maori
children, they are additionally disadvantaged by a lack of understanding of
the essentially European review and appeal processes. This provides a further
and strong argument for the implementation of restorative procedures in
schools based on the Maori community *hui* system.[42]

The limits to which school disciplinary procedures are subject are contained not only in education legislation but importantly they are embedded in
a Bill of Rights which offers protection to all citizens against the actions of
public authorities or bodies pursuing a public function.[43] Such rights may
only be subject to limitations which are justified in a free and democratic
society.[44]

NEW ZEALAND BILL OF RIGHTS ACT 1990

As public bodies, public schools are bound by the New Zealand Bill of
Rights Act 1990 (Bill of Rights). An inquiry conducted by the Commissioner
for Children soon after the enactment of the Bill of Rights found that the
guarantees therein exist in relation to students and the actions of school
authorities of public schools.[45] It is unclear whether the protections would
apply to students in private schools.

Still, there are decisions of the New Zealand High Court which suggest that agencies may be within the act's reach if, even though private, they are carrying out public functions.[46] While there are provisions of the act which could conceivably have application in the context of the responses of school officials to student misbehavior, they have not (yet) been invoked.

In addition to section 21, unreasonable search and seizure, and section 27 on the right to natural justice, there is section 9 on the right not to be subjected to disproportionately severe treatment or punishment and section 22 on the right not to be arbitrarily arrested or detained. The Bill was raised in argument in the case of *D v. M and the Board of Trustees of Auckland Grammar School* discussed next[47] where Smellie J held the disciplinary actions of the school were invalid as breaching provisions of the Education Act 1989 but he did not address the Bill of Rights argument except to remark that it "ploughed new ground."

SEARCH AND SEIZURE

In 2013 the Education Act 1989 was amended by the insertion of sections 139AAA–AAI which make new provisions for searches and the surrender and retention of property of students, effective from January 2014. The Minster of Education issued "Guidelines for the Surrender and Retention of Property and Searches" to provide advice to school principals, teachers, and boards of trustees on the principles underpinning the new provisions and the criteria for their operations.

Under the guidelines, essentially, teachers and authorized staff as defined under the act may require students to produce, reveal, or surrender an item or an electronic device. Before taking such actions, educators must have formed the belief on reasonable grounds that items in the possession of students are likely to endanger safety, or are likely to have detrimental effects on learning environments or are harmful. Importantly, "items" does not necessarily mean physical things but can include electronic information stored on computers or mobile phones.[48]

The Guiding Principles are set out in the guidelines as:

1. All schools are required to provide safe physical and emotional environments for students and staff (NAG 5);
2. Parents, students, and the public have a legitimate expectation that school environments are to be free from drugs, weapons, alcohol, and cyber-bullying;
3. In exercising the powers giving by Parliament in the new legislation, school administrators must act reasonably, in good faith, and in the least intrusive manner to achieve safe environments; and

4. Because of the protection afforded by section 21 of the New Zealand Bill of Rights Act 1990 school officials must be able to justify their actions as reasonable and necessary to ensure safe environments.[49]

CASE LAW—APPLICATIONS FOR JUDICIAL REVIEW FOLLOWING SCHOOL DISCIPLINE

Pursuant to the Judicature Amendment Act 1972[50] the High Court of New Zealand has the jurisdiction to review decisions made by persons in the exercise of statutory powers and public functions. In the first Application for Judicial Review concerning a school's disciplinary actions, following the inception of "Tomorrow's Schools,"[51] the High Court was clear in expressing its reluctance to become involved in education matters. In *Maddever v. Umawera School Board*, referring to the Education Act 1989, Williams J wrote:

> The legislation is informed by the democratic belief that responsibility is the great developer of the citizenry and that issues of local educational administration are best left for resolution through the individuality of local communities. A tendency to always turn to the law for resolution of these matters would be unwise and inappropriate.[52]

However, Jack Maddever had not been excluded from the school. Rather, his parents took action solely on their belief that the principal had not handled the matter of his discipline in a satisfactory matter. It is thought that the Williams J may have been influenced in his decision by the trivial nature of the incident leading to the parental action.

In subsequent cases the courts have shown no such reluctance and have been ready to intervene when the allegations were of breaches of natural justice. The first two which were of significant impact were *M & R v. S and Board of Trustees of Palmerston North High School*[53] and *D & S v. M and Board of Trustees of Auckland Grammar School.*[54]

In both of the preceding cases the High Court undertook a comprehensive examination of the legal requirements of school exclusions. In both cases, the judges emphasized the overriding requirement as fairness to students and the need to adhere to whatever requirements the circumstances of the individual cases called for in pursuance of that aim.

In *M & R*, the challenge was to the suspension of a group of high school boys who had been caught drinking alcohol on a school ski trip.[55] McGechan J was critical of the rector of the school who had applied the school policy on a "zero tolerance" basis in concluding that the boys' behavior amounted to "gross misconduct" pursuant to section 13(1) of the act. His Honor wrote that in his view the school had a responsibility, in considering actions which had such dire consequences for the students and their educational opportunity, to take all the circumstances into account. He said that the statutory approaches:

> are designed for the protection of children. They are not to be sacrificed to administrative or disciplinary efficiency, or some supposed need for absolute certainty. Results must not be fixed they must instead be fair. [56]

He continued:

> Is the misconduct striking and reprehensible to a point where it warrants removal from school, despite resulting individual damage? All the individual circumstances must be weighed. There are no absolutes. [57]

He allowed the students' applications and overturned the rector's decision to exclude.

In *D & S v. M and the Board of Trustees of Auckland Grammar School*[58] the student was suspended for possessing cannabis and his challenge was also successful, the judge finding that the principal based his decision on an error of fact.

The following cases continue staunchly upholding principles of natural justice in their scrutiny of the actions of school principals and boards of trustees. *Boviard and Another v. J Suing by his Litigation Guardian*[59] was a decision of the New Zealand Court of Appeal on appeal by the school authority. Keane J in the High Court had quashed the decision of the Principal of Lynfield College to suspend the respondent, a sixteen-year-old student.

Despite proceeding with their appeal, the principal and Board of Trustees of the College made it clear that they did not intend the outcome to affect the position of the student, who was reinstated following the High Court decision, and would continue at the college. In the underlying dispute the boy was suspended on two occasions, first for possession of marijuana paraphernalia, and second for misbehavior while on a school trip.

The Application for Judicial Review concerned the second suspension and alleged a breach of natural justice on the part of the school principal. The allegation, upheld by the High Court, was that the boy and other students who had been present on the school trip had been asked to make admissions of misconduct without their parents having first been advised and being given an opportunity to be present.

Keane J based his decision on his interpretation of the purpose of suspension as set out in section 13(c) of the Act and Rule 7 of the Suspension Rules,[60] and by reference to section 221 of the Children, Young Persons and Their Families Act 1989 which renders inadmissible any statement made by a child in the absence of being told of their rights and the presence of an adult.

The Court of Appeal disagreed. In the view of the judges, the overriding obligation is on principals to act fairly and "what is required to meet that obligation will depend on the facts of the particular case." But they added "there is no rule of law that a principal must involve parents prior to making a decision to suspend in every case."[61] It seems that the judges were influenced by the fact that in neither of the two leading cases did the absence of parental involvement meet with any "adverse comment."

In *D v. Havill and the Board of Trustees of Western Springs College*[62] the High Court again upheld a student's Application for Judicial Review on the ground that there had been a breach of natural justice. Andrews J, in line with the previous cases, emphasized that school disciplinary matters must be dealt with in accordance with principles of natural justice and what it requires depends on the facts and circumstances of each case.

The most recent successful quest by a student for High Court review of a suspension is *"A" v. Hutchinson and The Board of Trustees of Green Bay High School*,[63] a dispute over the suspension and exclusion of a fourteen-year-old boy with Asperger syndrome. It is of interest to note that in addition to Judicial Review, the applicant raised the issue of discrimination in breach of 56(1) of the Human Rights Act 1993, in common with the Australian case of *Purvis on behalf of Daniel Hoggan v. State of New South Wales (Department of Education and Training)*.[64] The Applicant did not pursue this line of reasoning, though.

It is abundantly clear from the jurisprudence that the courts are vigilant in ensuring that school authorities adhered to natural justice and to hold judicial challenges to be warranted where there is evidence of breach. It is also clear that judicial intervention, while reminding those exercising their legislative power to exclude a student of the strict obligations which accompany such a step, does little in terms of furthering educational goals and creating safe education environments for all children. It could be argued that litigation assists predominantly the economically advantaged and knowledgeable, and does little for the less acquainted with such judicial processes.

It is suggested that law, policy, and guidelines should lead schools to a more holistic view of the management of student behavior and to look particularly at community responses in the terms of restorative practices.

BEHAVIOR MANAGEMENT

Adopting restorative approaches instead of the more punitive and exclusionary response to school discipline develops a more positive whole school culture. Restoring relationships rather than attributing blame and exacting retribution are an effective response to relational aggression type behaviours. Bullied students just want the bullying to stop and tend to be less worried about making sure the bullies are punished.[65]

New Zealand schools and education authorities are starting to pay serious attention to alternative approaches to school misbehavior.[66] This is in recognition that the deficiencies of traditional approaches to school discipline in relation to student engagement, student behavior, and safety of the school community, weigh heavily against the disadvantages to the students concerned, school cultures, and to society as a whole.

According to the Ministry of Education website, in its guidelines for behavior management, school culture strongly influences student behavior. It directs school authorities to take proactive steps considering a range of strategies for managing student behavior such as school-wide programs, targeted programs, alternatives to stand-downs and suspensions, and the development of teaching staff toward this aim. The website gives some examples of restorative and mentoring programs which may be implemented based on "solving" behavioral problems rather than "blaming."[67]

Approaches which are alternative to the traditional retribution regimes have at their heart the notion of restoration of relationships, responsibility for and consequences of misbehavior, and a whole community approach to school safety. They are not a soft option. In the traditional retributive approach to student misbehavior it is too easy for it to become "the school's fault" and as with imprisonment in the criminal justice system, there is very little requirement or opportunity for the "offender" to face up to the harm caused rather than just be removed from society or from the school, in the case of education.

In 2007 the Commissioner for Children commissioned a report "Respectful Schools: Restorative Practices in Education"[68] in which the researchers considered alternative approaches used in some New Zealand state schools. The schools which were the subject of this study have implemented restorative practices which aim to change whole school cultures by building values or philosophies based on inclusion, repair, and reintegration, with strong supporting networks.

Initially, restorative practices in schools were based on restorative conferences, similar to those instituted earlier in the criminal justice system in response to youthful offenders. These practices are seen as a way of responding to serious behavioral problems by bringing together all involved to find ways to acknowledge wrongdoings, repair the harms, and find ways to reintegrate wrongdoers back into their communities.[69]

The report also discovered other strategies being employed by school authorities such as the use of mini-conferences, restorative classrooms to manage "in-class" problems, and restorative "thinking rooms" where students are able to work through themselves what happened and how they may respond constructively. Of the fifteen schools studied, the majority of teachers interviewed found considerable value in adopting the strategies, in terms of both reduction of exclusions and improvement in student retention and achievement, and in the school atmosphere generally.[70]

The teachers in these schools did acknowledge setbacks to their programs due to factors such as staff changes, insufficient staff training, and lack of staff commitment. The teachers attributed many of the hurdles to a lack of resources. Although there was considerable variation in the strategies used in these schools, they were all underpinned by the common principles and values of respect, relationship building, inclusion, achievement of each student according to their abilities and affirmation of achievement, and a celebration of diversity.

Subsequent to this report, in 2010 the Commissioner for Children conducted a comprehensive review into school safety in New Zealand.[71] The summary report "Responsive Schools"[72] summarizes the key messages from the research. As well as aiming to provide a valuable resource for schools in the area of behavior management particularly in response to peer conflict and bullying, it points to exemplary practices which have been implemented in schools. In this respect the introduction to the report notes:

> The case study schools have all worked over time to build a strong culture and ethos of school community. They demonstrate that the only programmes that are effective in addressing the problems of violence and aggression in schools are those that alter the school environment rather than focus solely on the bullies and victims.[73]

The summary report begins with the proposition that bullying behavior and violence in schools are whole school issues which require a whole school approach.[74] After considering the "successes" of the case study schools, the summary report sets out enablers and barriers to school safety which it identified. The enablers are essentially based on the involvement of whole school communities, teachers, parents, and students in introducing strategies for all and having a shared understanding and consistency in relation to appropriate and inappropriate behavior.

The study found that barriers to school safety are the implementation of reactive measures and zero tolerance policies which rely on school exclusion rather than zero tolerance attitudes to violence and bullying. Importantly, the report considered it imperative for educators to use prevention and intervention strategies designed to focus on the whole school climate as the most crucial contributing factor in promoting or inhibiting student misbehavior such as bullying.

Contemporaneously with the publication of this research, the Ministry of Education introduced its "Positive Behaviour for Learning Action Plan"[75] which was heralded as a major shift in the management of disruptive behavior in schools. This publication strongly recognizes the link between student behavior and the ability of all children to learn.

"The plan" recognizes that while the media focuses on the small number of incidents of severe misbehavior in schools, students' learning and school communities are impacted on to a much wider extent by low level disruptive acts of antisocial behaviors. Primarily, the plan aims to provide the support for school personnel and parents to reduce the barriers to learning that are posed by disruptive behavior of children.

The plan, which has five themes, is intended to implement the measures addressing these themes between 2010 and 2014. First, the key programs and activities are based on a school-wide and restorative approach. Second, early identification of behavioral patterns and support for at risk children are emphasized. Third, programs aimed at ensuring equal access for Maori, and programs which enhance cultural identity and support for the engagement of Maori "*whanau.*"[76]

Fourth, the plan identifies individualized services and "interagency collaboration" in the case of moderate to intense needs when behavior puts children and others at immediate or serious risk. Importantly, this provides for a large range of supporting activities related to student behavior management, particularly those which provide proactive support for all involved in school communities, teachers, students, and parents.

Fifth, it includes a review of legislation, regulations, and practices with the aim of reducing suspensions of children between the ages of five to eleven.

The plan is still at the early stages of inception.[77] Success in terms of better learning environments and improved student engagement in learning resulting in a lift in student achievement are still to be assessed. The extent to which these aims materialize may only be measured over time but there are many indications, in both research and practice, that a new approach to behavioral problems facing school communities is imperative.

CONCLUSION

Schools in New Zealand today, as elsewhere, are facing a multitude of problems relating to their students' engagement in learning and their behavior. Educators must manage many competing obligations. Clearly, educators have a duty to maintain safe educational environments which are conducive to learning and which are safe for all members of school communities. This is a responsibility imposed on school authorities by a considerable amount of legislation and policy.

It is clear that educators must act when threats emerge. However, if the actions educators take involve exclusions from schools, there are important considerations, the uppermost of which is the right of students to education. There are strict guidelines governing the actions of school officials that are imposed by legislation and case law.

Whatever the particular form of school exclusion, and despite legislation providing for alternative education, in reality any exclusion interrupts a child's education temporarily and, in many cases, permanently. Evidence suggests that disengagement from schooling is a significant precipitating factor in the incidence of juvenile offending and engagement with the criminal justice system.[78] Maori are particularly vulnerable.

Increasing attention is being paid to alternative options aimed at encouraging student engagement in their schools based on research demonstrating that best results occur in schools where there is a dual focus on behavior and academic achievement. At a national level in New Zealand, the Positive Behaviour for Learning: Action Plan 2010–2014 was updated in 2013.

In terms of managing student behavior there is a recognition that the way in which children behave in schools is strongly influenced by school culture. In the context of bullying, there is new attention being paid to the attitudes and behavior of staff as having the potential for either a positive or negative influence.

Insofar as violence may still happen despite the presence of preventative approaches, school authorities need to have processes in place to safeguard the rights of all members of their school communities and must know how to deal with it when it occurs. Importantly, such behavior is now recognized as a breach of the human rights of the victims and of whole school communities.

New Zealand schools are self-managing and able to make their own decisions as to the programs and processes they put in place to manage student behavior. Many authorities are now adopting whole school approaches based on a values system and school philosophies, agreed on by their whole school communities, and based on notions of responsibility, respect, and relationships.

These approaches are referred to as restorative practice with the focus on proactively working to change school communities, rather than react to specific incidents. Many of these programs embrace indigenous community processes in recognition of New Zealand's bicultural, and increasingly multicultural, nature. A wide variety of programs are operating in New Zealand schools, many of which are detailed in the two recent studies undertaken by the Office of the Commissioner for Children.[79] While the results of these are encouraging with regard to regulating student behavior, there is a long way to go:

All the courts or probation schemes on earth can never effectively correct the faults of the child as long as there remain the faults of those who deal with children in the home, schools, in neighbourhoods—in the community itself.[80]

KEY POINTS

The overriding consideration in all school discipline and the legislative ability of a school to search students and seize their property is a school's responsibility for a safe educational environment.

This requires a careful balance between an individual student's right to education and the safety of the whole school community.

Students have successfully challenged school disciplinary actions and courts have imposed a high standard of proof on schools to show that the misconduct is so "striking and reprehensible" to warrant exclusion. This is particularly the case in relation to students with learning and behavioral difficulties.

There are now strong moves toward approaches based on pro-action rather than reaction in the context of student behavior, for example: the Positive Behaviour for Learning Action Plan 2010–2014; and restorative practices aimed at respect and responsibility and based on the Maori "hui" community justice concept.

NOTES

1. §3Education Act 1989.
2. §§ 155,155[A] Education Act 1989.
3. §35A Education Act 1989.
4. §21 Education Act 1989.
5. http://www.educationcounts.govt.nz/statistics/schooling/homeschooling.
6. The very small number of children who are being home schooled was reduced from 0.8 percent from 2001–2010 to 0.7 percent from 2011–2013. Ibid. For a discussion on home schooling in New Zealand see S. Varnham, "My Home, My School, My Island: Home Education in Australia and New Zealand," *Public Space: The Journal of Law and Social Justice* 2, Art 3(2008): 1–30.
7. For the Office of Education Review, see http://www.ero.govt.nz; see also http://nzcurriculum.tki.org.nz (about the curriculum).
8. [2003] HCA 62.
9. [2014] NZHC 253.
10. [2014] NZHC 253, at para [69]. This case is discussed in this chapter.
11. [2003] UKHL 9.
12. Forty-three complaints in 2009, see "Disabled Children's Right to Education," Human Rights Commission, (2009): 7–8.
13. http://www.hrc.co.nz/2014/high-court-decision-welcomed.
14. s139A Education Act 1989. For material containing practical advice for parents and caregivers on school discipline, see N. Darlow, *Schools and the Right to Discipline: A Guide for Parents and Caregivers*, 5th ed. (Wellington Community Law Centre, 2011).
15. J. Caldwell, "Judicial Review of School Discipline," *New Zealand Universities Law Review* 22 (2006): 240–70, 244.

16. §15 Education Act 1989.

17. §17(1)(c).

18. As contained in § 3 Education Act 1989, and set out in Art. 29(1) United Nations Convention on the Rights of the Child.

19. http://www.minedu.govt.nz/NZEducation/EducationPolicies/Schools/StanddownsSus-pensionsExclusionsExpulsions.

20. n19. "Guidelines for Principals/Boards of Trustees on Stand-Downs, Suspensions, Exclusions and Expulsions," Ministry of Education.

21. n19.

22. www.educationcounts.govt.nz.

23. G. Maxwell and J. Carroll-Lind, "Impact of Bullying on Children" Office of Commissioner for Children Occasional Paper No. 6 (1997).

24. J. Carroll-Lind, "School Safety: An Inquiry into the Safety of Students at School," Office of the Children's Commissioner, New Zealand, (2009), 40.

25. For example, PLINFO which provides free legal advice to parents and children on education matters.

26. "Trends in International Mathematics and Science Study" (TIMSS 2006/07 cited in the Executive Summary), viii; J. Carroll-Lind, "School Safety: An Inquiry into the Safety of Students at School," Office of the Children's Commissioner, New Zealand (2009).

27. The guidelines may be found at n19.

28. Pursuant to §§ 60A and 61(2).

29. NAG 5(i)–NAG 5 (iv).

30. However in this context it is important to note the decision of the New Zealand Court of Appeal in *Boviard and Another v. J Suing by his Litigation Guardian* [2008] NZCA 325 in which it was stated, per O'Regan J (para 56) that there was no statutory requirement for the principal to consult with parents before deciding to stand-down or suspend a student.

31. In this respect, see the amendments to the Education Act 1989 inserted by Sections 139AAA–139AAI which relate to searches and confiscation of property in schools, and the "Guidelines for the Surrender and Retention of Property and Searches" released by the Ministry of Education in January 2014 to assist Principals and Boards of Trustees in their actions.

32. It is important to remember however that in respect of personal injury, common law actions for compensatory damages are barred in return for compensation payable under the state-run accident compensation regime. A duty of care may be owed however in respect of mental harm.

33. Health and Safety in Schools Code of Practice, 2007, Ministry of Education, www.minedu.govt.nz./EducationSectors/StateSchools/HealthAndSafety/HealthAndSafetyInS-chools.doc. For further information on health and safety see chapter 6 EOTC Guidelines, http://eotc.tki.org.nz/EOTC-home/EOTC-Guidelines.

34. *Tavita v. Minister of Immigration* [1994] 2 NZLR 257, in which Cooke J of the Court of Appeal remarked that there are some international obligations that are so manifestly important that no Minister should fail to take them into account.

35. Set out in J. Carroll-Lind, "Responsive Schools: Summary Report," March 2010, Office of Children's Commissioner, 7–8.

36. Ka Hikitia–Accelerating Success 2013–2017 the "strategy to rapidly change how the education system performs so that all Māori students gain the skills, qualifications and knowledge they need to enjoy and achieve education success as Māori." www.minedu.gov.nz.

37. Statistics available at www.educationcounts.govt.nz.

38. L. Smith, "Te Rapunga i te Ao Marama: The Search for the World of Light" in *The Issue of Research and Maori*, Monograph No. 9, Research Unit for Maori Education, University of Auckland, quoted in R. Garden, "School Discipline in New Zealand: Legal and Policy Implications" (1992). Paper presented at the Annual Conference of the Australia and New Zealand Education Law Association (ANZELA), Rotorua, New Zealand, October 2012.

39. J. Scheurich, "Colouring Epistemologies: Are Our Research Epistemologies Racially Biased?" *Educational Researcher* 26 (4) (1997): 4, 13, quoted in Garden R "School Discipline in New Zealand: Legal and Policy Implications," Paper presented at the Annual Conference of

the Australia and New Zealand Education Law Association (ANZELA), Woteva Next! Legal and Social Challenges in Education, Rotorua, New Zealand, October 3–5, 2012.

40. Refer "Positive Behaviour for Learning Action Plan: Get It Right for Maori." It should be noted that while there are Maori language immersion schools or *kura kapapa*, within the state system, only a small minority of Maori children have access to them.

41. R. Bishop et al., "Te Kotahitanga: Addressing Education Disparities Facing Maori Students in New Zealand," *Teacher and Teaching Education* 25 (2009): 87.

42. Considered in the report of the "Commissioner for Children: Respectful Schools: Restorative Practices in Education," (2007), S. Buckley and G. Maxwell, Office of the Commissioner for Children and the Institute of Policy Studies, School of Government, Victoria University of Wellington, New Zealand . See section "Behavior Management."

43. s 3 New Zealand Bill of Rights Act 1990. It should be noted however that while this is not supreme law it has been accorded high status by the New Zealand courts.

44. n 43, §5.

45. *Re Strip Search at Hastings Boys' High School* [1009–1991] 1 NZBORR 480.

46. For example, *Wilson v. White* [2005] 1 NZLR 189.

47. [2003] NZAR 726.

48. Sections 139AAA-139AAI Education Act 1989, Education (Surrender, Retention, and Search) Rules 2013 and "Guidelines for the Surrender and Retention of Property and Searches" January 2014, Ministry of Education, www.minedu.govt.nz.

49. "Guidelines for the Surrender and Retention of Property and Searches," January 2014, Ministry of Education, www.minedu.govt.nz, at 2.

50. Note the 2012 Review of the Judicature Amendment Act 1908: Towards a New Courts Act (the government has yet to implement its policy following this report). http://www.lawcom.govt.nz/sites/default/files/publications/2012/11/nzlc_r126_judicact_web.pdf.

51. The government policy of 1988 which introduced self-governing schools by way of the Education Act 1989.

52. [1993] 2 NZLR 478 at 508.

53. [2003] NZAR705 (HC).

54. [2003] NZAR726 (HC).

55. Although the decision of McGechan J was in 1990 the case was unreported until 2003 in [2003] NZAR 705.

56. *M & R v. S & Board of Trustees of Palmerston North Boys High School* (2003) NZAR 705, 718 (decided December 5, 1990), 725.

57. n56, p. 725 per McGechan J.

58. [2003] NZAR 726.

59. [2008] NZCA 325 (27 August 2008).

60. The Education (Stand-Down, Suspension, Expulsion & Exclusion) Rules 1999.

61. n59, para [63] per O'Regan J.

62. [2009] NZHC (September 30, 2009).

63. [2014] NZHC 253. It must be noted that at the time of writing it is reported that the Board of Trustees is planning to appeal this decision to the New Zealand Court of Appeal.

64. [2003] HCA 62

65. J. Carroll-Lind, "School Safety: An Inquiry into the Safety of Children at School" (2009) Office of the Children's Commissioner, xii. Retrieved from the website of the Commissioner for Children http://www.occ.org.nz.

66. See S. Varnham, "Getting Rid of Troublemakers: The Right to Education and School Safety—Individual Student vs School Community," *Australia and New Zealand Journal of Law and Education* 9(2) (2004): 53–69. For an Australian discussion on traditional and new approaches to school discipline, see S. Hemphill and J. Hargreaves, "The Impact of School Suspensions: A Student Wellbeing Issue," *ACHPER Healthy Lifestyles Journal* 56(3/4) (2009): 5–11.

67. See S. Varnham, "Seeing Things Differently: Restorative Justice and School Discipline" *Education and the Law* 17(3) (2005): 87–101.

68. S. Buckley and G. Maxwell, Office of the Commissioner for Children and The Institute of Policy Studies, School of Government, Victoria University, Wellington (2007).

69. S. Buckley and G. Maxwell, "Respectful Schools: Restorative Practices in Education. A Summary Report" (2007) Office of the Children's Commission and The Institute of Policy Studies, School of Government, Victoria University of Wellington (2007), 7.

70. n69,18.

71. *School Safety: An Inquiry into the Safety of Children at School"* can be retrieved from the website of the Commissioner for Children, http://www.occ.org.nz.

72. J. Carroll-Lind, "Responsive Schools," published by the Commissioner, March 2010. Summary Document to the Report in n69.

73. Ibid, p. 1

74. n69, 27.

75. The plan and its accompanying material may be accessed at http://www.minedu.govt.nz/ theMinistry/EducationInitiatives/PositiveBehaviourForLearning.

76. *"Whanau"* is the Maori term for extended family. For a discussion of the impact of culture on student behavior and learning environments and student discipline in New Zealand, see A. H. Macfarlane, "Discipline, Democracy and Diversity: Creating Culturally-Safe Learning Environments," Presentation at Taumata Whanonga, Wellington, March 16–17, 2009.

77. Note the Positive Behaviour for Learning PB4L Action Plan Update 2013. http:// www.minedu.govt.nz/NZEducation/EducationPolicies/SpecialEducation/OurWorkPro-gramme/PositiveBehaviourForLearning/~/media/MinEdu/Files/TheMinistry/PositiveBehavi-ourForLearning/PB4LUpdate2013.pdf.

78. See, for example, M. Weissman et al., "School Yard or Prison Yard: Improving Outcomes for Marginalized Youth," Center for Community Alternatives Justice Strategies, Syracuse, New York, US, April 2005; His Honor Judge A. J. Becroft, Principal Youth Court Judge, New Zealand Youth Court. Te Kaiwhakawa Matua o Te Kooti Taiohi o Aotearoa & Rhonda Thompson, Research Counsel to Principal Youth Court Judge, 'Youth Offending: Factors that Contribute and How the System Responds." Paper delivered at the symposium "Child and Youth Offenders: What Works," Office of the Commissioner for Children, Wellington, New Zealand, August 22, 2006.

79. J. Carroll-Lind, "School Safety: An Inquiry into the Safety of Students at School" and its summary report "Responsive Schools" (2010); and S. Buckley and G. Maxwell, "Respectful Schools: Restorative Practices in Education" (2007), Office of the Commissioner for Children and The Institute of Policy Studies, School of Government, Victoria University, Wellington. Both may be downloaded from the website of the Office of the Commissioner for Children, www.occ.govt.nz.

80. Benjamin Lindsey, Judge of the Juvenile Court in Denver (1909).

Chapter Three

The Changing Shape of Misdemeanor in Singapore Schools

Mui Kim Teh

Singapore is a tiny multicultural island city-state with a governing structure patterned on the British system of parliamentary government. Although small,[1] Singapore has an estimated population of five million people, comprising mainly Chinese, Malays, and Indians. Once a British colony, Singapore gained independence in 1965 and it has since become one of the most prosperous countries in South East Asia.

The legal system of Singapore, from 1819 when it was founded by Sir Thomas Stamford Raffles until its independence in 1965, was based on English legal traditions, practices, case law, and legislation. However, since independence, there has been a gradual move away from relying solely on English law for guidance and a greater tendency to consider the laws and legal systems of other commonwealth jurisdictions, such as Australia and Canada.

When adopting legal principles, the guiding principle is that it must be compatible with Singapore's economic, multicultural, social, and other conditions (Tan and Chan, 2007). To further establish its independence, in 1993, the right to appeal to the Privy Council was abolished, with the Court of Appeal becoming the highest appeal court of the land.

The Constitution (1999 Rev Ed) is Singapore's supreme written law; any law enacted after the Constitution that is inconsistent with it is void. The important doctrine of separation of powers, which maintains that there are three distinct functions of government, is contained in the provisions delineating the powers and functions of the various organs of state, namely, the legislature, the executive, and the judiciary.

Legislative power in Singapore lies in the Parliament, which consists of both elected and nonelected Members of Parliament (MPs). The nonelected

51

MPs do not enjoy voting rights on constitutional amendments, money bills, and votes of no-confidence in the Government.

There are two different categories of nonelected MPs: Non-Constituency Members of Parliament (NCMPs) and Nominated Members of Parliament (NMP). NCMPs are appointed from the candidates who have polled the highest percentage of votes among the "losers" in the general election; NMPs, in contrast, are nonpoliticians with distinguished contributions to society who have been nominated to provide a greater variety of nonpartisan views in Parliament (Tan and Chan, 2007).

The head of the Executive is the Elected President, and the Cabinet, under the leadership of the Prime Minister, is collectively responsible to the Parliament. Arguably, because members of the Cabinet are drawn from the MPs, effectively, there is no complete separation of powers between the Executive and Legislature.

The judiciary administers the law with complete independence from the Executive and Legislature. With the abolition of the jury system in 1970, judges are the arbiters of both law and fact in Singapore. Judicial power is vested in the Supreme Court (comprising the Singapore Court of Appeal and the High Court) as well as the Subordinate Courts. The Court of Appeal, which hears both civil and criminal appeals from the High Court and the Subordinate Courts, is the final appellate court.

The other courts in Singapore are the Constitutional Tribunal, which hears questions about constitutional provisions, the Subordinate Courts (District Courts, Magistrates' Courts, Juvenile Courts, Coroner's Court, and the Small Claims Tribunal), which hear simple, specific, and complex cases, and the Family Court, which handles divorces, maintenance, custody, and adoptions.

As in many, if not most, jurisdictions, alternative dispute resolution (ADR) is also actively promoted as a means of dispute resolution for matters ranging from domestic and social conflicts to large-scale cross-border legal disputes. The main modes of ADR are negotiation, mediation, and arbitration. Additionally, to encourage a mediation culture in a multiracial and multireligious country like Singapore, the Community Mediation Centres Act (Cap 49A, 1998 Rev Ed) was enacted in 1997 to establish regional mediation centers and other smaller mediation venues to facilitate community mediation as an effective way of settling relational disputes (Tan and Chan, 2007).

Singapore is in a strategic location but lacks natural resources. To survive, it needs foreign capital, technology, and markets, along with "brainpower" to work within the economic system and to "nurture future-ready Singaporeans" (FY 2010 Committee of Supply Debate, 2010). In this way, education is a crucial concern for the nation and decisions on education matters (from the primary to university level) are made at a national level by the Ministry of Education, with policies being initiated to nurture students and shape future leaders to meet the challenges of an increasingly service- and knowledge-based economy (Teh and Stott, 2009; Teh and Chia, 2011).

Compulsory education was introduced in Singapore in January 2003 under the Compulsory Education Act (CEA) but covers only six years of primary education. A child of compulsory school age refers to one above the age of six years who has not yet attained the age of fifteen years. Under the CEA, it is a criminal offense if parents fail to enroll their Singapore-born children in government schools offering primary education (i.e., national primary schools offering public education) and to ensure their regular attendance in these schools.

The CEA ensures that Singapore citizens will at least acquire basic literacy and numeracy skills, as well as core values, a common educational experience, and national identity in their first six years of primary education. However, the CEA exempts children with special needs and those attending religious schools run by the Islamic Religious Council of Singapore.[2]

Against this background, the remainder of this chapter is divided into the following six substantive sections: student misconduct in schools; the most frequent forms of student misconduct; the application of due process to disciplinary methods; methods for dealing with student discipline; the link between teachers' duty of care and student misconduct; and emerging issues.

STUDENT MISCONDUCT IN SCHOOLS

Judging from the media, internet resources, and informal chats with teachers, the global picture of student misconduct in schools appears to be an increasing concern, not just in Western countries but in Asian countries as well.

What constitutes misconduct? In Singapore schools, where the author was engaged in teaching and a management position, the kinds of student misconduct that were prevalent in the 1980s and 1990s were mainly inattentiveness, poor concentration, clowning, restlessness, talking out of turn, disturbing others, not completing homework, and failing to study for tests. Over the past few years, media coverage of incidents of bullying and shootings in the United States and Britain suggests that student misconduct has moved to the level of crime and violence, not just simple classroom misdemeanors.

In recent meetings in Singapore with school principals, teachers,[3] school counselors and psychologists, and parents of school-aged children, face-to-face interviews were conducted to ascertain the answers to the following questions:

1. What is the state of misconduct of students in Singapore schools?
2. What is the most frequent form of student misconduct?

3. What are the various methods of dealing with student discipline?
4. What are the emerging issues in relation to student behavior?

The purpose of using face-to-face interviews was to gain insights into the subjective and lived experiences of the interviewees. The findings, which were meant to be a reflection of the issues being considered in this book, are not necessarily representative, but do offer a useful indication of some of the issues that have emerged in the contemporary scene of schools.

THE STATE OF STUDENT MISCONDUCT IN SINGAPORE SCHOOLS

There was a considerable overlap of the kinds of student misconduct high-lighted by the interviewees. A variety of those interviewed commented that the definition of "misconduct" is very different from the past. Misconduct now, they responded, is not just confined to misdemeanors in the classroom, within school compounds or even outside of schools, but has extended to "invisible spaces" in the form of cyber-bullying and text messages.

According to the interviewees, the trends in misconduct in Singapore schools comprise mainly the following:

- From primary to secondary schools—online offenses in the form of slandering and bullying through the use of blogs, email, and text messages. Another form of online offense is the posting of inappropriate sexual images.
- Bullying in the form of fighting (usually boys) and verbal attacks (usually girls). One teacher cited a bullying case where a child was stabbed with a pencil. Another teacher commented that students play practical jokes on new students under the guise of "ragging" but fail to appreciate the danger involved and how far they can go. Victims of such ragging can be bullied by being pushed into ponds or even toilet bowls.
- Bullying in the form of extortion, which is the result of gangsterism (mainly in neighborhood schools[4]). Schools that have this problem have to deal with police reports on a regular basis, sometimes even daily.
- Theft of mobile phones and cameras; and indirect theft, for example, using someone else's phone to download games.
- Disrespect for teachers in the form of showing defiance (rebutting the teacher rudely); playing with a mobile phone while the teacher is talking; being condescending to teachers.
- Willfully breaking school rules; for example, using personal IT devices (iPod, iPhone) during school hours; not following the dress code.
- Disobedience in the form of refusing to obey instructions from teachers.

- Forging parents' signatures in forms and reports.
- Students sleeping in class because they went to sleep late the night before.
- Teenagers clubbing at night, drinking. Teachers are seeing a trend where upper secondary students are doing this, not just pre-university students. [5]
- Sexual misconduct among students. This happens in both upper primary and secondary schools.
- In secondary schools, drugs and smoking.
- Truancy.
- Misconduct outside school, such as throwing things into people's homes after school; throwing cigarette butts into compounds, causing fires.

Interviewees offered some views on the reasons for the misconduct listed. In the case of bullying, a number considered it to be a way of expressing pent-up anger and frustration. One reason for the frustration is the inability to meet extremely high academic standards, such that clever students in classes become bullied. Children with special needs, such as autism and dyslexia, are often targets too. In the case of theft, the interviewees were of the view that many do it for the thrill of it, not out of need.

Some students are seen as condescending to teachers because they expect teachers to be experts in their respective fields. In this age of major technological advances, where information is so readily available, students show contempt if they believe that their teachers are not as knowledgeable as they think they themselves are.

Another issue is that late nights for students seem to be increasingly prevalent. The result is that it is not unusual for students to be fixed on their computers surfing the internet, playing games, or watching videos into the late hours. While it may have been unusual for students to fall asleep in class a decade or two ago, it is now an all-too-frequent occurrence.

It is sad that sexual misconduct among students appears to be on the rise. The counselors who were interviewed noted that some cases even led to sexually transmitted diseases, as children as young as eleven or twelve are engaged in consensual sex and girls are becoming more promiscuous. Teenage pregnancies are therefore becoming more and more common. One might argue that what students do outside school is not within the purview of the school, but culturally and morally, principals and teachers consider such conduct wrong.

The main reason given for the presence of drugs and smoking is that youths are increasingly influenced by the people they meet in games arcades. Yet, it was further pointed out that offenses in this area are probably not as serious as those occurring in western countries, because the punishments imposed by the Singapore courts serve as a strong deterrent. For example, under the Misuse of Drugs Act (2008), one faces the death penalty if caught with more than certain amounts of specified substances. The possession of weapons is also severely punished with lengthy prison sentences and caning.

THE MOST FREQUENT FORMS OF STUDENT MISCONDUCT

All Singapore schools have sets of school rules and regulations in their handbooks. While they are set out in different formats, the types of behavior that are deemed to be misconduct or categorized as offenses are very similar. In one school, the offenses are broken down into "Attendance-related offenses," "Misconduct-related offenses" and "Criminal and other very serious offenses." In another school, the list of offenses is categorized as "Attendance," "Conduct," "Theft/Damage of property," "Other serious offenses," and "Other offenses." Yet another school simply lists the offenses as "Minor," "Serious," and "Major."

The types of misconduct commonly listed in schools are: attendance; late coming; missing classes; leaving school without permission; truancy; improper attire and grooming; cheating on tests/examinations; not handing in work; open defiance and rudeness; forgery; disruptive behavior; obscene language; and using mobile phones without permission. Serious offenses typically include fighting/assault; bullying; physical or verbal threats; extortion and intimidation; theft and shoplifting; vandalism; substance abuse; smoking; and gangsterism.

In one school,[6] rules are set out in categories, with specific offenses listed in their respective categories. Possible actions taken by school officials are then spelled out clearly for the breaches of each offense. Table 3.1 is an example from one school.[7]

CARE AND RESPECT FOR SELF AND OTHERS

To care for others, one must be able to care for oneself by keeping healthy physically, mentally, and emotionally. Being respectful toward others is important to provide a pleasant environment for others to teach and learn.

Table 3.1 Offense: Absent from school/Leaving school without permission

No. of times	Possible Actions	Merit Points Deducted
1	Inform parents/Detention x 1	2
2	Inform parents/Detention x 1	4
3	Inform parents/Detention x 1 Counseling Session x 1	4
4	Inform parents/Detention x 1 Counseling Session x 1/Caning	4

Students who deny others their rights to have a conducive environment for study face the following consequences.

According to the interviewees, the most frequent forms of student misconduct are rudeness and defying teachers, bullying (including online bullying and maligning of teachers), vandalism, truancy, and being late for school. This is not a long list, considering the fact that there are many categories of offenses.

Misconduct of particular concern is bullying. However, it is not physical bullying that is particularly worrying, because it is perceived as a behavior

Table 3.2

Offense	Possible Actions	Merit Points Deducted
Disruptive behavior 1st & 2nd incidence	FT to inform parent/Detention x 3/Apology Letter/Reflection	–
Disruptive behavior 3rd incidence onward	FT to inform parent/Detention x 3/Apology Letter/Reflection	2
Leaving classroom without permission from teacher	Detention x 1	-
Open defiance and rudeness to teacher	Student to apologize to teacher in class/Parents informed/Caning for serious cases/Counseling by ST/FT//DM/3 x detention/Reflection	8
Using vulgar/objectionable language or gesture 1st incidence	Letter of apology/FT to inform parents. Detention x 3	4
Using vulgar/objectionable language or gesture Subsequent incidence	Letter of apology/FT to inform parents. Detention x 3	6
Possession of undesirable materials (e.g., pornographic material, chewing gum)	Parents informed/Materials to be confiscated. Detention x 3	6
Possession of undesirable materials (e.g., pornographic material) (Subsequent offense)	Parents informed/Materials to be confiscated/Caning (for boys)/CWO (for girls) Counseling/Close monitoring/Police involvement	10
Fighting, hooliganism, causing physical hurt to others, bullying	FT to inform parents/Caning (for boys)/ CWO (for girls)/Counseling/Police involvement/Letter of Undertaking to be signed by both student and parents/Expulsion if necessary	10
Smoking/Possession tobacco products or lighters	FT to inform parents/Detention x 3/Refer to HSA/Caning (for boys) CWO for girls.	10
Vandalism/Destruction of school property	FT to inform parents/Offender to pay for the damage, clear the graffiti and rubbish from the vandalized areas/Parent to sign letter of undertaking/Caning (for boys) or CWO (for girls) for serious cases/Counseling/Police involvement/Letter of Undertaking to be signed by both student and parents/Expulsion if necessary	6-10
Misbehavior in public that tarnishes the good name of the school	Parents informed/Close monitoring/Counseling/Barred from school activities and excursion/Detention x 3	6-10

management problem that should and could be handled by school officials. Rather, the main concern is internet bullying, especially the more subtle and insidious kind of emotional bullying that has now affected even teachers, who are sometimes the victims of internet slander. Perpetrators of this form of misconduct are often difficult to trace.

THE APPLICATION OF DUE PROCESS TO DISCIPLINARY METHODS

The Singapore government has always made it clear that the push for a global free-market and human rights must be balanced against the nation's need to preserve political and cultural autonomy; that the Western model of democracy is not appropriate for all; and "that nations must be allowed to develop their own forms of human rights; that is, which take the cultural context for its expression into account" (Gopinathan, 2001, 6). In this regard, the founder of the ruling People's Action Party (PAP) has taken the view that neo-Confucian ideology is the most appropriate alternative framework for socioeconomic and political organization (Lee, 1994). The style of government for a long time has therefore been paternalistic, authoritarian, and inflexible.

Since 1959, the PAP has won all elections and, to a large extent, it still remains an authoritarian state with strict curbs on freedom of expression, assembly, and association. Human rights observers have pointed to the denial of due process rights, draconian defamation laws, and tight controls on independent political activity[8] (Human Rights Watch 2009).

If on a national level the notion of due process is not given priority, the application of due process in schools is not very much different. There is an assumption that once school rules are broken, authorities have the prerogative to impose punishment. School handbooks only spell out the various offenses and the disciplinary measures that will be meted out for breaches.

It is immensely problematic gaining access to information from the Ministry of Education as to its policy on procedural due process in regard to acceptable punishment,[9] which is sad, given that Singapore has developed successful policy that could profitably be shared with other systems. Even so, the results of interviews revealed that, in practice, for serious offenses, school officials usually conduct some form of conferencing with parents and relevant parties to establish the facts before taking any action. Generally, though, students are expected to be familiar with school codes of behavior and must face the consequences should they break any rules.

METHODS FOR DEALING WITH STUDENT DISCIPLINE

School handbooks spell out the disciplinary measures for student misconduct with officials usually observing standard operating procedures when meting out punishments. The list below is not exhaustive, but sets out the most commonly used methods in schools:

- Counseling by school counselors or educational psychologists (see the REACH program later in this section).
- Informing parents of the misconduct and working together to correct student behavior. The mode of communication includes telephone calls from class and subject teachers as well as letters to parents.
- Reflections wherein students are made to write down what they have done wrong and why it is wrong.
- Punitive measures include:

  - Demerit points systems which may lead to deprivation of school awards
  - Disqualification from representing the school in competitions
  - Detention class; community service in the school
  - Suspension (rare)
  - Expulsion (rare)
  - Corporal punishment—caning (rare)

Of the methods listed here, suspension, expulsion, and corporal punishment are the more extreme strategies of school discipline or behavior management. The general view is that cases involving such forms of discipline are few and far between, and even if they are utilized, parents have no reason to protest, since the school rules make the punishment that is attached to any given offense clear from the outset.

Much controversy centers around the use of corporal punishment as a mode of punishment in Singapore. Most jurisdictions have banned corporal punishment. When the nation acceded to the 1989 Convention on the Rights of the Child, Singapore expressly declared that a child's rights, as defined in the Convention, shall be exercised with respect for the authority of parents, schools, and other persons who are entrusted with the care of the child.

Singapore added that article 19 does not prohibit the judicious application of corporal punishment in the best interests of the child (United Nations Human Rights Treaties, 2011). Nevertheless, school officials are given strict guidelines by the Ministry of Education on how and when to administer corporal punishment; it is used only as a last resort.

A tool that is available to school authorities when dealing with students with behavioral problems is the REACH[10] program. Under this program, school counselors obtain training, support, and helpline assistance from a multidisciplinary team comprising medical doctors, clinical psychologists, counselors, medical social workers, occupational therapists, nurses, and administrators.

REACH teams collaborate with school counselors to provide suitable school-based interventions to help these students (Institute of Mental Health, 2011). Many instances of misconduct are due to students suffering from severe emotional and behavioral problems. School counselors thus have this resource to provide suitable school-based interventions to help affected students.

THE LINK BETWEEN TEACHERS' DUTY OF CARE AND STUDENT MISCONDUCT

It is an accepted fact that school leaders owe students a duty of care. Generally, this duty of care refers to taking responsibility for the students' physical well-being while they are on school premises and negligence in doing so may result in liability. The question that arises is whether this duty of care extends to making sure that students do not misbehave.

An obvious link between the duty of care of teachers and student misconduct are to prevent bullying on school grounds and to respond to incidents of bullying. In doing so, school officials might avoid having to deal with claims for physical or psychological harm for their failure to prevent bullying.

Bullying is a problem that affects all schools at some point. The consequences for victims of bullying are far-reaching. Statistics in Britain show that at least sixteen children commit suicide each year because they have been the victims of bullying (Marr and Field, 2001). ChildLine, a phone counseling service for children in distress, concluded that "promoting a culture of decency within a school seems to be the bedrock on which real success depends. The role of the head teacher in this process appears to be pivotal" (Marr and Field, 2001, 149).

According to Bullying Statistics (2010), about 2.7 million students in the United States are bullied each year. One of the reasons for this huge number is because social networking has provided an entirely new environment for it to flourish. A very sad outcome of bullying is that of suicide, which is believed to be one of the leading causes of death among children under the age of fourteen (Bullying Statistics, 2010).

There is a common trend shown in incidents of bullying. These occurrences suggest that school authorities are usually not liable if students bully peers but are liable if, having knowledge of the bullying, they fail to act.[11] In Singapore, where the government is making unprecedented efforts to increase the population, children are seen as precious commodities. Parents, naturally, are thus becoming more and more protective of their own children.

The failure of educators to manage incidents of physical violence on their premises can be seen by these parents as a breach of the duty of care to provide safe learning environments for their offspring. For school officials to discharge their duty of care, it is important that they take active steps to minimize the risk of bullying by having systems in place, especially in the areas of monitoring, review, and enforcement of policies. Inactivity or insufficient activity may result in legal liability.

EMERGING ISSUES

All respondents indicated that student misconduct will get worse before it gets better. Many reasons were given but the lack of parental guidance was the most prominent. Parents fail to guide or discipline their children for a myriad of reasons, the most common of which are:

1. Home breakups, which often see children losing the motivation to behave and instead misbehaving by stealing, vandalizing, being defiant, being vulgar, and bullying.
2. "Neglect," where career-minded parents are so busy with work that they simply do not have the luxury of time to spend with their children, let alone discipline them. These children are often left in the care of live-in maids, grandparents, or childcare centers (which children do not see as authoritative figures or institutions) and when their parents do see them, they may overcompensate for their neglect by giving in to the children's demands.
3. The notion of human rights—due to globalization and the advance of internet technology, Singaporeans are now more aware of human rights issues. Under the guise of exercising their rights, then, students openly challenge teachers with the backing of better educated and more liberal parents. These parents often frown on disciplinary methods like detention, community service, or corporal punishment, which they deem to be cruel or demeaning.

A retired teacher who taught from 1965 to 2004 lamented that disciplinary issues are no longer what he used to experience as a teacher. In those days, "most parents supported the teachers when their children were disciplined for poor conduct" but now "teachers handle their charges gingerly to avoid complaints from over-protective and demanding parents. School heads fear parental fury and hence ban caning and scolding" (Ho, 2010, 12).

With decreasing parental influence and increasing online community influence, what are the emerging issues concerning student misconduct? This

question was posed to the interviewees who responded that the following
will be encountered increasingly:

- Using electronic devices during school hours in breach of school rules.
- Bullying (physical, internet, mobile phones).
- More aggressive behavior because of the influence of violent television programs, and arcade, computer, or video games.
- Declining morals and sexual misconduct.
- Inappropriate relationships between teachers and students.
- In single sex schools, homosexual behavior which, in Singapore, is considered culturally and morally unacceptable.

It is interesting to note that sexual misconduct is highlighted as one of the emerging issues. There appears to be a fear of the erosion of culture due to globalization. Globalization has opened up world markets with the growth of numerous worldwide networks, and technology plays an important role in people's lives. This permeability of communication and information may have contributed to a shift in the sexual values of the younger generation. Society has become more "open," and it is no surprise that sexual misconduct in schools is beginning to be a worry.

As suggested by the interviewees, the difficulty here lies not so much in the blatant sexual misconduct of teachers, but rather in the innocent (in intent) and friendly touching of students by teachers, or in situations where teachers knowingly have relationships with students outside school hours. Those situations put school leaders in a quandary.

Another emerging issue identified by the interviewees is cyber-bullying. Cyber-bullies can reach their victims simply with the click of a mouse or a button on a phone, and they can often escape from legal or disciplinary consequences.

School leaders are often placed in difficult positions because they do not see themselves as legally able to discipline students for internet offenses occurring outside of school. Yet, some of these offenses can have serious effects on both teachers and students during school hours in terms of emotional and psychological harm. Perhaps a basis for schools to intervene in cyber-bullying cases would be the fact that such misconduct does interfere with student learning in the school, albeit indirectly. Thus, more steps may need to be taken to encourage victims of cyber-bullies to report incidents of such bullying so that educators can take appropriate actions to manage problems that arise.

CONCLUSION

In Singapore, like most Asian countries, there is a culture of showing respect for elders and for authority. Asians believe that insofar as the age of persons equates with maturity and knowledge, elders are entitled to respect for these attributes; this respect is often given according to the hierarchical order (Sandhu, 1997). Besides age, official position is also regarded as a form of social status. Students are expected to treat teachers with respect because teachers are deemed to be experienced, knowledgeable, and wise professionals who are qualified to address both scholastic and personal matters (House and Pinyuchon, 1998).

There are signs of an erosion of such cultural values. It is reported that students are willing to challenge teachers, show defiance, or assert their rights even if it means showing disrespect. This is, for some, a worrying trend, but more research needs to be undertaken to ascertain the true picture. Often, the more dramatic but less widespread and less frequently committed kinds of student misconduct are given prominent media attention.

Where discipline is concerned, Singapore is one of the few countries still permitting corporal punishment. As a safeguard, the Ministry of Education sets out strict policy and guidelines for the administration of corporal punishment.

Under Ministry guidelines, only principals are permitted to use corporal punishment. Many jurisdictions and even some parents in Singapore frown on this form of discipline. Still, one might argue that if teachers are expected to act *in loco parentis* in relation to pupil safety, then they should similarly be allowed to act *in loco parentis* when disciplining children. This may mean allowing school authorities to use discipline methods that children best understand and those could possibly include corporal punishment.

An interesting development in Singapore is the setting up of REACH,[12] a collaboration among schools, voluntary welfare organizations, the medical profession, and the National Council of Social Services to help identify and support students with emotional and behavioral difficulties, as well as related mental health problems. The school counselors who were interviewed commented that, with the implementation of this community-based program, they have seen positive progress in their students.

Singapore is a relatively safe place. To date, there is no evidence of violence or unrest in Singapore that one might see in schools in, say, the United States or the United Kingdom. Although the types of student misconduct that occur today may be different from those of the past, there seems to be little evidence of misdemeanors escalating to the extent of those in some Western systems. The difficulty for Singapore educators lies not in identifying the right disciplinary responses to student misconduct, but rather in man-

aging the shift in cultural values, where authority is being increasingly challenged.

The final point concerns sexual misconduct. This is another difficult issue, because school leaders and their teachers often rely on their own moral
convictions to judge whether student misbehavior is reprehensible or not.
Arguably, some judgments (at the school level) may fall way below generally accepted norms.

This chapter has reviewed the current state of misconduct in Singapore
schools, emerging trends, and the various methods employed by schools to
deal with student discipline. There has been a discernible move toward counseling, parental involvement, and community interventions, while punishment has been relegated to a last-resort measure. This is perhaps appropriate,
for, as Ziglar (1989) comments:

> Discipline . . . includes everything you do to help your child learn. . . . We
> need to understand that discipline is something you do for a child. Punishment
> is something you do to a child when discipline fails. . . . The purpose of
> discipline is positive—to produce a whole person, free from the faults and
> handicaps that hinder maximum development. (p. 193)

There is no question that Singapore, despite its cultural imperatives and no-
nonsense approach to misdemeanor, has not been immune from a trend in
many systems of escalating misbehavior and declining respect for authority.
It is even more important in Singapore, though, than in many other countries,
in light of the need to maintain high standards of academic excellence and
achievement, that ways are found to deal with the malady of misconduct in a
way that will lead to sustainable measures to maintain a safe and effective
learning environment.

KEY POINTS

We have seen how the societal context in a nation like Singapore is having an
adverse impact on the lives of children. Diminishing parental involvement
and discipline, and almost unbridled access to negative influences from
across the globe are leading to situations where student learning is being
seriously affected. There are several points from this research that are worth
reinforcing.

First, there needs to be a renewed emphasis on discipline rather than
punishment. It may be necessary for schools, as far as possible, to educate
parents in the need for sound discipline to support the school.

Second, multidisciplinary support mechanisms, such as REACH, are
more likely to have an effect on complex problems than simplistic, one-size-

fits-all intervention strategies, especially if those strategies are merely sanctions and punishment.

Third, cyber-bullying is probably the greatest malady we currently face amongst children, and it may be necessary for schools to become involved more than they presently are. The effects of such bullying are sometimes catastrophic, and it may not be legally defensible to allow this activity to go without forceful intervention, even if it is technically outside the school, since it affects children's lives considerably within the school.

NOTES

1. Singapore only has a total land area of 699 km^2 and 193 km of coastline.
2. However, such designated schools, as with other mainstream schools, have to prepare their Singapore students for the national primary school leaving examination.
3. These include current teachers, retired teachers, and teachers who have left the profession.
4. Neighborhood schools are perceived as ordinary schools with low academic achievement and a greater percentage of students from low social economic status. Popular schools, on the other hand, are considered better because of high achievement and are perceived as having more holistic educational programs. However, the reality is that popular schools may perform better academically because parents can afford tuition classes or these schools accept mainly brighter students. In fact, the quality of teaching in both popular schools and neighborhoods does not differ greatly and many neighborhood schools similarly have very good holistic educational programs.
5. Pre-University Education prepares students for the GCE "A" Level examination at the end of the two-year junior college or three-year centralized institute course. Pre-university students range from the age of seventeen to nineteen.
6. The table and wording below are obtained from the school at the time of writing and have not been edited.
7. The more serious actions are highlighted in bold in the table to signify the seriousness of the offense. The following acronyms are also used in the table:
FT: Form Teacher
ST: Senior Teacher
DM: Discipline Master
CWO: Corrective Work Order
HAS: Health Services Authority
8. Interestingly, in the latest General Election in 2011, the final results saw a 6.46 percent swing against the PAP from the 2006 elections to 60.14 percent, its lowest since independence. It was also the first time a Group Representation Constituency was won by an opposition party (Singapore General Elections, 2011).
9. There is no freedom of information legislation in Singapore and school principals, quite reasonably given their context, are largely unwilling to comment on even basic factual information. A written request for information from the Ministry of Education on this subject was simply met with a courteous reply with reference to the following website on the Ministry's Social and Emotional Learning values, http://www.moe.gov.sg/education/programs/social-emotional-learning/.
10. REACH (Response, Early Intervention and Assessment in Community Mental Health) was started in 2007 under the National Mental Health Blueprint, serving the mental health needs of school-aged children and adolescents. The program has been progressively rolled out in the north, south, and east school zones, led by the Institute of Mental Health (IMH) in collaboration with the Ministry of Education (MOE), voluntary welfare organizations (VWOs), family doctors and the National Council of Social Services (NCSS). In March 2011, this

program was extended to the west school zone as well, making it a nation-wide program (Institute of Mental Health, 2011).

11. See *Davis v. Monroe County Board of Education*, 526 U.S. 629 (1999); *Haines v. Warren* (1987) Aust Torts Reports, 80-115; New South Wales Court of Appeal.

12. See the section in this chapter on dealing with student discipline for more details.

REFERENCES

Bullying Statistics. (2010). Retrieved from http://www.bullyingstatistics.org/content/bullying-statistics-2010.html.

Compulsory Education Act (Singapore) (Chapter 51). (2003).

Constitution of the Republic of Singapore. (1965).

Convention on the Rights of the Child. (1989). Retrieved from http://www.ohchr.org/EN/ProfessionalInterest/Pages/CRC.aspx.

FY 2010 Committee of Supply Debate (2010). 1st Reply by Dr Ng Eng Hen, Minister for Education and Second Minister for Defence on Strengthening Education for All. Retrieved from http://www.moe.gov.sg/media/speeches/2010/03/09/fy-2010-committee-of-supply-de.php.

Goh, C. B., and S. Gopinathan. (2008). "The Development of Education in Singapore since 1965." In S. K. Lee et al. (2008). (Eds.). *Toward a Better Future: Education and Training for Economic Development in Singapore since 1965* (pp. 12–38). The International Bank for Reconstruction and Development/The World Bank.

Gopinathan, S. (2001). "Globalisation, the State and Education Policy in Singapore." In Tan J., Gopinathan, S., How, W.K. (Ed) (2001). *Challenges Facing the Singapore Education System Today* (pp. 3–17). Prentice-Hall.

Ho, K. L. (2010). Today Voices. *Where's the discipline?—Too Often, School Leaders' Hands Are Tied with Dealing with Errant Students.* August 12, p. 12.

House, R. M., and M. Pinyuchon. (1998). "Counseling Thai Americans: An Emerging Need." *Journal of Multicultural Counseling and Development* 26, 194–204. In R. Mathews, (2000). "Cultural Patterns of South Asian and Southeast Asian Americans." *Intervention in School and Clinic* 36(2): 101–104.

Human Rights Watch (2009). World Report Chapter: Singapore. Retrieved from http://www.hrw.org/world-report/2009/singapore.

Institute of Mental Health (2011). *News Release: A Complete Mental Health Community Network for Children and Adolescents Islandwide.* 14 March 2011. Retrieved from http://www.imh.com.sg/news_events/newsroom.html.

Lee, K. Y. (1994, October 6). "Confucian Values Helped Singapore Prosper." *The Straits Times*, 6 October. In Gopinathan (2001). Globalisation, the state and education policy in Singapore. In Tan J., Gopinathan, S., How, W. K. (Ed). (2001). *Challenges Facing the Singapore Education System Today*, 3–17. Prentice-Hall.

Marr, N., and T. Field. (2001). "Bullycide, Death at Playtime." (Success Unlimited, Didcot, Oxfordshire, Great Britain 2001, 256). In Hay-Mackenzie, F. (2002). *Tackling the Bullies: In the Classroom and in the Staffroom*. Paper presented at the Australia and New Zealand Education Law Association 11th Annual Conference: Legal Risk Management Safety Security and Success in Education, Brisbane (October 2–4), 119–159.

Misuse of Drugs Act Chapter 185 (2008).

Sandhu, D. S. (1997). "Psychological Profiles of Asian and Pacific Islander Americans: Implications for Counseling and Psychotherapy." *Journal of Multicultural Counseling and Development* 25, 7–21. In Mathews, R. (2000). "Cultural patterns of South Asian and Southeast Asian Americans." *Intervention in School and Clinic*, 36(2), 101–104.

Singapore General Elections (2011). Wikipedia. Retrieved from http://en.wikipedia.org/wiki/Singaporean_general_election,_2011.

Tan, E., and Gary Chan. (2007). The Singapore Legal System. Singapore Academy of Law. Retrieved from http://www.singaporelaw.sg/content/LegalSyst.html.

Teh, M. K., and K. Stott. (2009). "Singapore." In Russo, C.J. and DeGroof, J. (2009). (Eds.) *The Employment Rights of Teachers: Exploring Education Law Worldwide* (pp. 173-187). Lanham, MD: Rowman and Littlefield Education.

Teh, M. K., and S. M. Chia. (2011). "Singapore" in the edited book "Balancing Freedom, Autonomy, and Accountability in Education" published by Wolf Legal Publishers of Tilburg, The Netherlands and edited by Charles L. Glenn, Jan De Groof and Cara Stillings Candal (in press).

The United Nations Human Rights Treaties. (2011). *Declarations, Reservations, Objections and Derogations*. Retrieved from http://www.bayefsky.com/docs.php/area/reservations/state/155/node/3/treaty/crc/opt/0.

Ziglar, Z. (1989), *Raising Positive Kids in a Negative World.* New York: Ballantine Books.

Chapter Four

The United Kingdom—Managing Behavior to Optimize Learning because "Every Child Matters"

Patricia Walker

It is generally accepted that student misconduct is a problem worldwide, which makes it a fruitful topic of investigation for the comparative educationalist. Even so, there are three preliminary issues around which researchers must proceed with caution.

Firstly, comparativists cannot promise to provide ideal solutions, but believe that there is much to learn from one another as individual societies struggle to deal with common issues and common concerns. Secondly, it is important to note that a possible barrier to understanding one another is the problem of nomenclature since terminologies we believe we hold in common, may have entirely different understandings in different societies, countries, and contexts.

It is essential therefore that we define terms. For instance, in the United Kingdom (UK) the term "student misconduct" is not used in the school sector. Instead, the phrase "pupil behavior" is more usual. As such, this chapter discusses the levels of severity of "misconduct" together with a broad range of strictures along a continuum of universal to targeted sanctions, together with what we believe is equally important, targeted support.

Third, it is important to bear in mind that any national system of education is the expression of the nation-state and a manifestation of that nation's priorities, values, beliefs, and customs together with expectations of what represents desirable and undesirable behaviors in that society: the school is a microcosm of the individual society. Whilst bearing in mind that the objective of this book is to identify best practice from other societies, we need to be mindful of the dangers of cultural transplantations.

Researchers cannot just pick and mix behaviors which may be embedded in cultural norms and mores which differ from our own. It is worth remembering the words of the great Isaac Kandel:

> The comparative approach demands first an appreciation of the intangible, impalpable, spiritual and cultural forces which underlie any education system: *the factors and forces outside the school matter even more than what goes on inside.*[1]

In the UK, all teachers in state maintained schools are required to have one-year postgraduate qualifications in the practice of teaching in addition to three-year bachelors (first) degrees or a four-year education degrees incorporating qualified teacher status (QTS). This requirement is present because there is a presumption on the part of professionals that effective teaching and learning, together with good classroom management, will result in good pupil behavior. In addition, expectations of good and bad behavior are seen in a broader framework of social and emotional needs.

The Every Child Matters (ECM) agenda expressed in the white paper of the same name[2] and supported in legislation by the Children Act of 2004,[3] governs all aspects of working with children. Its aim is for every child, whatever their background or circumstances, to have the support they need to achieve what are known as "the five outcomes," namely: be healthy; stay safe; enjoy and achieve; make a positive contribution; and achieve economic well-being. This approach requires every Local Authority (LA) working with its partners, through Children's Trust partnerships, to find out what works best for children and young people in its area and acting on it.

Children and young people (CYP) are to be involved in this process, and the Office for Standards in Education, Children's Services, and Skills (Ofsted) inspectors, will ensure they have been when making their judgments: all schools must benchmark their working practices against this practice.

It is central to the thinking of the entire CYP workforce that youth's behavior is a visible expression of their well-being; a tangible and often quantifiable indicator of their health, security, and happiness. Politicians, academics, and other professionals believe that, "A child who is well fed, properly housed and adequately cared for has the capacity to engage with education and a broader community. A child who is hungry, abused, neglected or parentified cannot be 'in the moment' of a classroom."[4] This is the UK way in general and in this London borough specifically.

It therefore follows that the dominant ideology in the United Kingdom is not about stifling inappropriate behavior but supporting productive behavior through engagement with other CYP services to support the whole child, families, and schools. It is underpinned by robust research, a plethora of guidance for the children's workforce and informed by engagement and consultation with all stakeholders not least children and their parents.

Against this background, the remainder of this chapter examines legislation governing discipline in schools; the state of student misconduct in schools; the most frequent forms of student misconduct; powers to discipline; the application of due process to disciplinary methods; the link between teachers' duty of care and student misconduct; and emerging issues. The chapter concludes by identifying a tension between national and local government on the ways forward to support managing pupils' behavior in schools.

LEGISLATION GOVERNING DISCIPLINE IN SCHOOLS

The Education and Inspections Act 2006[5] requires every school to have "a behavior policy," the details of which can be found in sections 88–96 of the law. The Labour government had set out its commitment to improving school discipline in a white paper, "Higher Standards, Better Education for All"[6] which commitments the 2006 Act carried forward, including the establishment of a statutory power to enforce school discipline and more specific measures relating to excluded pupils[7] and to parental responsibility for the behavior of children.[8]

Under this approach, the UK government expects pupils to show respect to teachers, other staff, and one another; parents to encourage their children to respect the authority of the school in respect of discipline; head teachers to create a culture of respect by consistently supporting the authority of staff; governing bodies and heads to deal with allegations against teachers and staff in a way that protects the pupil and the subject of the allegation; and every teacher to manage learning and improve children's behavior.

Statutory duties are devolved from the central government to the Local Authority (LA) which, in their turn, devolve some of their authority to local school officials. In their turn, schools are managed by governing bodies consisting of the head of the school, parent governors, staff governors, community governors, and LA governors. Governing bodies meet once a "term"; there are three terms in every academic year to consider the operational management of schools. One of the important duties of governing bodies is, in consultation with head teachers, to determine school behavior policies.

Governors are responsible for ensuring that, following national guidance applying to all maintained schools (community; foundation; voluntary; community special; foundation special; maintained nursery), pupil referral units and nonmaintained special schools set general principles informing behavior policies.[9] The governors must consult head teachers, school staff, parents, and pupils when developing these principles.

Head teachers are responsible for developing and operationalizing the behavior policies of their schools in the context of this framework. Head teachers must decide on what standards of behavior are expected of pupils and how they will be achieved, school rules, disciplinary penalties for transgressing them, and equally important, rewards for good behavior with a view to "securing that pupils complete any tasks reasonably assigned to them in connection with their education" and which, in addition, promotes self-discipline, respect for others, and proper regard for authority; prevents bullying; and leads to an acceptable standard of behavior by pupils.

Head teachers can include measures in the policies regulating the behavior of pupils when they are off school sites or not under the control of staff members such as during their journeys to and from school or at work experience placements. School behavior policies are not intended to be implicit but must be explicit in written form in formal documents publicized to staff, pupils, and parents and purposefully brought to everyone's attention at least once a year.

THE STATE OF STUDENT MISCONDUCT IN SCHOOLS

Troubled behavior of pupils is also very disconcerting to heads and class teachers; it also is a source of extreme anxiety and stress to those affected. Moreover, pupils' disruptive behavior is detrimental to the successful learning and enjoyment of learning, of their fellow pupils. Most troubling is that the unacceptable behavior of pupils is deeply damaging to the well-being and thriving of the pupils themselves, affecting their social relationships as well as their emotional and mental health.

Currently in the United Kingdom both the popular—that is, mainstream—and the specialist press, seem to be preoccupied with education issues. The Conservative/Liberal Democrat coalition appears to have a very different philosophy of education from the previous Labour (Socialist) administration with education matters consequently hitting the headlines.

There seems to be widespread concern about "pupil behavior" which is said to be no better than satisfactory in almost a fifth of England's secondary (high) schools. Government statistics published by the DfE report that Ofsted (the government's school inspectors) judged pupil behavior in 18.4 percent of secondaries, as either satisfactory or inadequate. [10] In 0.1 percent of secondaries, it was judged to be inadequate, the lowest descriptor used by the inspectorate. [11]

The government minister responsible for schools expressed concern that almost one in five secondaries was rated no better than satisfactory for behavior although these figures are better than the previous year when pupil behavior was satisfactory or inadequate in 21.3 percent of secondaries. However, 54.5 percent of high schools in England had behavior that was good and in 27.1 percent it was outstanding.

Interestingly the Inspectors rated pupil behavior in primary (elementary) schools more highly judging behavior to be outstanding in 37.9 percent, good in 55.8 percent, below good in 6.2 percent, and inadequate in just 0.1 percent. It is also interesting to note that standards of behavior across the country show huge variations. In some areas of the country, just a quarter of secondary schools have pupil behavior which is either good or outstanding. In other areas, all schools' behavior has been rated as good or outstanding, a range that appears to be similar to the one from the previous year.

THE MOST FREQUENT FORMS OF STUDENT MISCONDUCT

According to Ofsted, the behavior of pupils which remains a serious concern for many schools and other settings is usually that of boys: their behavior can trouble others, affect the climate of the learning community, and disrupt their own and others' progress. In addition, it is worth pointing out, that in the United Kingdom overall, considerable emphasis has been put on inclusion in recent years. [12]

An Ofsted report, "Special Educational Needs and Disability: Towards Inclusive Schools," [13] confirmed that pupils with emotional, behavioral and social difficulties (EBSD) are the most difficult group for schools to manage. This is a dilemma for schools which embrace inclusivity since there can be a tension between meeting individual needs and the efficient education of all other children.

School authorities are required to document those behaviors leading to the most extreme penalties, namely, permanent exclusion and fixed-term exclusion. The table here sets out the main reasons for exclusion and whether permanent or temporary. Figures are the most recent available from the DfE. [14]

During the 1990s the rate of permanent exclusions in England was such that in 1997 the newly elected Labour government determined to reduce numbers by a third before 2002. When that target was met schools were subsequently encouraged to continue to reduce permanent exclusions. The National Strategies program "put exclusion at the heart of planning and provision" [15] and numbers of permanent exclusions became a performance indicator.

One reason for exercising vigilance in respect of exclusion is because it has become clear that certain groups of students are much more likely to be excluded than others; for instance, pupils with special educational needs (SEN) are eight times more likely to be permanently excluded than other pupils and are more likely to be given fixed term exclusions than other

Table 4.1

Reason for exclusion	Number of pupils (fixed-period in parentheses)
Physical assault against a pupil	980 (64,030)
Physical assault against an adult	580 (16,370)
Verbal abuse/threatening behavior against a pupil	250 (13,410)
Verbal abuse/threatening behavior against an adult	630 (69,190)
Bullying	50 (5,100)
Racist abuse	20 (3,900)
Sexual misconduct	100 (3,350)
Drug and alcohol related	370 (8,770)
Damage	80 (7,630)
Theft	140 (6,460)
Persistent disruptive behavior	1,660 (78,760)
Other	870 (54,410)
TOTAL	**5,730 (331,380)**

pupils. Of the 331,380 fixed term exclusions in 2009–2010 (see table 4.1), 217, 490 applied to children who had SEN, that is, almost two-thirds of all excluded children.[16]

Other children disproportionately represented in the excluded population are Irish travelers, Black Caribbean, Gypsy/Roma, and Mixed Caribbean. Indeed, Black Caribbean pupils are nearly four times more likely to be permanently excluded than the population as a whole.

Children who are eligible for, and claiming, free school meals are four times more likely to be excluded than other children.[17]

The previous data indicate that it is essential to explore the root causes of misbehavior: it is not just an educational problem; society has created these children in that the underlying causes are societal, usually in the family environment. It is a collision of factors difficult to distinguish or disentangle the multiple points of influence in a young person's life. Risk factors in the lives of children can impact on their cognitive behavioral and emotional development, as well as on their mental health, well-being, and educational attainment.

Pupil misbehavior has recently achieved a very high degree of public attention and scrutiny in the United Kingdom. As such, pupil misbehavior is commanding a great deal of space in newspapers, both mainstream and specialist publications, particularly bullying. As the data here demonstrate, bullying is one of the most common forms of misconduct damaging both victim (in terms of anxiety and low self-esteem) and the perpetrator, on whom it has a brutalizing effect contributing to mental ill health. Most worryingly, it seems that young people are finding new ways to inflict damage on one another.

Nearly one in five UK youngsters has been the victim of cyber-bullying,[18] with girls affected more than boys, according to research by Anglia Ruskin University in which academics questioned almost five thousand young people aged between eleven and nineteen: Among respondents, 18.4 percent admitted they had been subjected to cyber-bullying, saying the experience had damaged their confidence and mental health and resulted in absence from school and cessation of socializing outside of school. Twenty-two percent of girls questioned said they had suffered from this kind of bullying while 13.5 percent of boys had faced it. Sixty-six percent of the young people questioned said they had witnessed cyber-bullying or known someone who has been a victim.

As for whether they would seek help with cyber-bullying, the majority of student respondents replied that they would not, fearing it would exacerbate the problem and hoped they could deal with it themselves. Others said they would probably seek help from parents and friends.

Most online interactions are neutral or positive. Even so, researchers believe the internet provides a new means through which children and young people are bullied. There is a growing interest in the United Kingdom in researching the use of social media among young people with pressure on host sites and government agencies to address the bullying issue before it gets worse.

Bullying in classrooms does not exist only among pupils. *The Guardian* reported the story of a science teacher who lost control and hit a fourteen-year-old pupil about the head with a 3-kg weight while shouting "die, die, die."[19] The experienced teacher had been provoked by pupils who called him a "psycho" and "bald-headed bastard" during a lesson in July 2009. The pupils had previously planned to "wind up" their teacher so his reaction could be caught on a camcorder being used secretly by a girl in the class. The footage was then to be passed around the school as a way of humiliating the teacher. The court believed him to be a fundamentally decent person and cleared him of attempting to murder the boy or intending to cause him serious injury, but the man is now banned from teaching for life.

POWERS TO DISCIPLINE

Teachers and teaching assistants as well as other staff in the school with responsibility for pupils have the power to discipline those whose behavior is unacceptable or who fail to follow reasonable instructions. According to the circumstances, this power could apply to behavior outside the school as well as within.

School staff also have the power to search pupils for items banned from school but must do so with the pupils' consent.[20] If a staff member suspects a pupil has weapons, alcohol, illegal drugs, or stolen items their possessions can be searched without the need to obtain consent. Teachers and other school staff are authorized to impose penalties for undesirable behavior: such disciplinary measures take many forms.

EXPULSION AND SUSPENSION

In the United Kingdom, "expulsion" is usually referred to as *exclusion* and can be *permanent* or *fixed term* while in other countries it may be referred to as "suspension." Whether heads exclude children permanently or for a period of time depends on the severity of the misconduct. Both penalties are discussed together in this section. Exclusion is not a penalty to be exacted lightly and to demonstrate that is so, the LA has a statutory duty to provide advice and guidance on the exclusion process to schools, governors, parents, and other interested parties. It also must ensure that schools have regard to the DfE's guidance when making decisions on exclusion and administering the exclusion procedure. The department's guidance applies to all maintained schools and Pupil Referral Units (PRUs).

Academies, by virtue of their funding agreements with government, must also have regard to the guidance; procedures followed by Academies therefore should not depart significantly from those in the guidance without good reason. As of September 2007, LAs have a legal duty to make full-time provision from the sixth school day of a permanent exclusion; school authorities have the legal duty to make full-time provision from the sixth school day of fixed-term exclusions.

Because there are many negative consequences resulting from periods of exclusion, not only for the excluded individuals but also their peers, school staff, and parents, guidance from the DfE encourages school leaders to consider alternatives to this penalty. For minor transgressions the articulation of a teacher's disapproval or disappointment may be all that is required; for behavior involving the use or possession of banned items, the retention or confiscation of a pupil's property or in extreme cases the disposal of it is seen as a reasonable measure. For more serious cases of misconduct the DfE guidance suggests:

Intervention measures are employed for pupils who are at risk of being excluded. Under this process pupils remain on school rolls but are educated at other educational settings such as a pupil referral unit (PRU). These PRUs are designed so that individuals are provided with alternative provision to meet their specific needs. Such provision could include using the Common Assessment Framework (CAF) to engage the support of other agencies, such as the national health service (NHS) special educational needs (SEN) providers.

Restorative justice is used so that individuals who have caused loss or suffering to other children, or damage to property, are required to make good the loss or repair damage.

Mediation can involve parents or family members, other children and their families, residents from the community surrounding the school, and local priests or imams or elders from temples, churches, and mosques.

Internal exclusion, refers to situations where disruptive children are removed temporarily to separate them from others, to quiet rooms or therapy rooms where they can safely express their emotions.

Managed moves refers to moves to other schools, a voluntary process whereby the respective heads of mainstream schools can negotiate moves at times or places which are in the best interests of pupils; these moves could also be to PRUs or an alternative provider.

THE APPLICATION OF DUE PROCESS TO DISCIPLINARY METHODS

Procedures on Hearings and Appeals

When pupils are excluded for fixed terms, their parents have the right to challenge the decisions of head teachers either at a Governors Review Meeting or via a letter to the governors, depending on the length of the exclusion. Where pupils are excluded permanently, the governors must meet to review the exclusion either agreeing with the action of the head teacher and so uphold the exclusion or deciding that pupils should be reinstated.

If the governors uphold the exclusions, the parents or caregivers have the right to appeal against an independent panel constituted and clerked by the LA. The decisions of independent appeal panels are binding on all parties except that parents and governing bodies may appeal to the High Court for a Judicial Review if they believe that an order is unlawful or that a reasonable panel would not have arrived at the same outcome.

The inspectorate (Ofsted) is currently consulting on changes to tighten up issues around due process, since, as mentioned above, preventing children from engaging in education is a violation of their democratic right in this country. The proposed procedures are as follows:

- when deciding to exclude pupils, head teachers should ensure that records are kept of their actions and of those of other staff;

- further guidance will be given to schools on dealing with breaches of rules relating to the appearance of pupils;
- revised guidance on what actions school authorities should take following fixed-period exclusions;
- new material on reintegration interviews;
- changes to the guidance on what actions should be taken following a permanent exclusion;
- revised guidance on behavior relating to parenting orders and contracts;
- revised guidance on looked-after children;[21]
- revised model letters;
- new guidance for exclusions panels on combined hearings and factors to consider when deciding whether to uphold an exclusion;
- schools and local authorities to offer parenting contracts as an earlier intervention—before excluding pupil;
- schools will be able to apply for parenting orders where pupils "seriously misbehaved," regardless of whether they were excluded; and
- penalty notices are to be available for parents of pupils who are found during the first five days of an exclusion in a public place during school hours, without reasonable justification.

The Application of Corporal Punishment

All school staff have the power to use "reasonable force" to restrain pupils and prevent their doing harm to themselves, other children and staff members, or school (or other) property. There is special guidance on using restrictive physical interventions with children and adults who display extreme behavior, particularly in association with learning disability or autistic spectrum disorder.[22]

However, corporal punishment (CP) in British state schools, and in private schools receiving any element of public funding, was banned by parliament in 1987.[23] CP was not banned in private schools until much later; until 1999 in England and Wales; until 2000 in Scotland; and not until 2003 in Northern Ireland.[24] Since Scotland and Northern Ireland have a number of differences in terms of practice what follows refers to England (and Wales) only.

Throughout the 1960s and 1970s there had been a determined campaign by a group of anti-CP individuals in the teaching trade unions and the Labour party which controlled most of the urban local education authorities (LEAs). Politicians of the then ruling Conservative Party at Westminster had mostly remained in favor of CP, but they eventually were won over. On July 22, 1986, the House of Commons voted for total abolition by 231 votes to 230—a majority of one single vote.[25]

The state education system in England and Wales used to be highly de-centralized such that there were always wide variations of practice between schools even in the same area. The only rule laid down by central government was that all formal CP was supposed to be recorded in a punishment book. The 100 + LEAs in England and Wales either formulated their own rules or chose not to have any. For instance, in some places the tawse was specified instead of the cane.[26]

Only one LEA required all canings for both sexes, even at secondary level, to be applied to offenders' hands and not to their buttocks. On the other hand caning of the hands was strongly discouraged as potentially injurious in others and elsewhere it was ruled that girls, unlike boys, must not be caned at all, though they could be slapped with the open hand.

Some LEAs mandated the number of strokes, from three to six; most decided that the act be performed in private while others insisted on a witness. About half of all LEAs said that only women teachers could punish girls, but only Inner London and Oxfordshire, determined that only men could cane boys. Some forbade the caning of girls other than on their hands while explicitly stating that boys could be disciplined either on the hands or on the clothed buttocks. Some prohibited teachers from hitting pupils' heads or "boxing their ears."

Other LEAs restricted the number of staff permitted to inflict CP such as the head teacher and those specifically delegated by him or her. At least one LEA laid down that the punishment must follow as soon as possible after the offence while others insisted on a cooling-off period before discipline was administered.

However organized, it was seen by many as an act of barbarism and further, did not succeed in preventing misconduct. However, in September 2011 a survey commissioned by the Times Educational Supplement (TES),[27] revealed that the majority of parents and pupils think teachers should have the power to be tougher with unruly students. Almost half of parents and nearly a fifth of children believe caning should be brought back to the classroom in cases of very bad behavior.

THE LINK BETWEEN TEACHERS' DUTY OF CARE AND STUDENT MISCONDUCT

Government guidelines warn local authorities that if they seek to minimize the number of exclusions of pupils for disruptive or violent behavior they must have regard to their duty of care to other pupils and the health, safety and welfare of the workforce. Traditionally, the term *in loco parentis* was used to describe the duty of care that teachers had toward pupils. The effect is that teachers have a duty to take the same reasonable care of pupils that a parent would take in those circumstances.

In loco parentis originally embodied the nineteenth century common law principle that teachers' authority was delegated by parents so far as was necessary for the welfare of children. A British court held, in 1893, that "the schoolmaster is bound to take such care of his pupils as a careful father would."[28]

Over time, a teacher's duty of care to individual pupils was understood to be influenced by, for example, the subject or activity being taught, the age of the children, the available resources, and the size of the class. Moreover, from case law it has come to be recognized that the standard of care expected is the application of the ordinary skills of a competent professional—that is, the skill and care of a reasonable teacher. If it can be shown that a professional acted in accordance with the views of a reputable body of opinion within their profession, the duty of care will have been met even though others may disagree.

It goes without saying that a breach of the duty of care by a teacher could be construed as negligence. A teacher's employer could be liable for the payment of damages in compensation to a pupil who is injured as a result of negligence. Negligence could also arise if there is a serious failure to prevent harm to a child arising from, for example, pupil bullying.

There is also a statutory duty of care—The Children Act 1989 Section 3 (5) defines the duty of care to the effect that a person with care of a child may do all that is reasonable in the circumstances for the purposes of safeguarding or promoting the welfare of the child.[29]

When issues arise concerning safeguarding or promoting the welfare of children, teachers should take into account the ascertainable needs and wishes of the children as individuals. These needs and wishes should be considered in the light of pupils' ages, understanding, and any risk of harm. Contractual duties of teachers are expressly defined in the School Teachers' Pay and Conditions Document (STPCD),[30] maintaining good order and discipline among pupils and safeguarding their health and safety, both when they are authorized to be on the school premises and when they are engaged in authorized school activities elsewhere.

In considering the harm that may befall pupils the emphasis for teachers is to prevent it from occurring rather than to focus on pursuing those children who may cause harm. It is understood from robust research, that children who cause harm to others through their undesirable behavior are also invariably victims themselves; of bad parenting, of neglect, of delayed development, or of stress, anxiety, or other mental and emotional lack of well-being.

It is for this reason that preventative measures are in all cases preferred to punitive actions ex post facto. The ECM agenda has been embraced nationally and guides working with children and their families. As a nation, the

United Kingdom has made significant investment in preventative work including pastoral care systems with child care professionals in addition to teachers providing mentoring and counseling. There are social workers and mental health workers in schools as well as designated police—not for crowd control but for educational purposes, as well as an emphasis on rights and responsibilities and the growth in parenting programs.

EMERGING ISSUES

As touched on previously, pupil behavior is the principal educational issue exercising public comment in the United Kingdom. Journalists on the right of the political spectrum are preoccupied with what the *Sun* newspaper termed "broken Britain" to describe a perceived widespread decay in society, and the summer riots, though brief, were terrifying to most Britons as they watched buildings burned and shops looted over a few August days. The Prime Minister, David Cameron, uses the phrase and it has passed into common use despite being fiercely contested by many teachers, academics, and politicians. He describes a "slow-motion moral collapse" in Britain, while ruling out race, poverty, and government spending cuts as factors, refusing Labour's demand for a public inquiry looking into the causes of disaffection.[31]

The Education Bill 2011[32] is the government's first major Education Bill published January 27, 2011, implementing the proposals set out in the White Paper—"The Importance of Teaching"—published in November 2010[33] and is interesting here, in that it gives major attention to measures relating to pupil misconduct such as:

- Extending the power of members of staff to search pupils without their consent for items that have been, or are likely to be, used to commit offenses or cause injuries to the pupils or another, or damage property, and to search for items banned under the school rules.
- Makes changes to the process for reviews of permanent exclusions.
- Repeals the duty on schools to give twenty-four hours' written notice of a detention to parents.
- Repeals the duty on all schools to enter into a behavior and attendance partnership with other schools in their areas.
- Repeals the duty on local authorities to appoint a school improvement partner in each maintained school.
- Repeals the power of parents to make complaints about schools to the Local Commissioner.
- Extends the Secretary of State's power to close any school he decides are eligible for intervention, rather than (as at present) only those deemed by Ofsted to be in need of special measures.

As a measure of how important Ofsted is taking the issue of "student misconduct" the arrangements for inspection in England and Wales are currently being consulted upon in documentation from the DfE.[34] Schools will also face inspections from Ofsted without prior warning, under an overhaul of the rules set out by Michael Gove, the Education Secretary. Their inspectors will also be expected to make more "no notice" visits to schools, to carry out spot checks at establishments where discipline is causing problems.

Although a framework for unexpected inspections was established in 2009, since then only five schools have been visited without a twenty-four-hour notice period. The Government has stated that in those schools with very bad behavior problems more "no notice" inspections are needed so that it becomes unacceptable for schools to tolerate persistent serious problems.

CONCLUSION

Perhaps it is inevitable in an advanced, relatively wealthy, and democratic society that individuals will express and espouse a range of views, approaches, philosophies, and strategies across a wide continuum of positions. In the United Kingdom at the moment, in respect to education generally and student misconduct specifically, there is an unusually high degree of polarity. Moreover, it is the government and the LAs which are representative of the poles apart.

As seen here, the LAs are wedded to the ECM philosophy of focusing on the best outcomes for the child in terms of being healthy (including emotionally), achieving, and being safe, of looking at the child not as he is but as what he can be; to seek out the causes of disruptive behavior and understand that they are often a cry of fear, or a cry for help; and of early intervention strategies focusing on supporting the child and the family.

The national government, on the other hand, is following a strategy emphasizing punishing behavior, exacting penalties including bringing criminal charges against children who accuse their teachers of wrongdoing; taking away duties from the LA in terms of partnership working with schools on behavioral issues, claiming to give power back to teachers in the classroom, yet inspecting them without notice, taking powers away from parents but investing greater powers in the Secretary of State to make unilateral decisions to close down schools.

In this climate it is not clear who will come out the winners. But unless central and local government can work together and support one another, it is not difficult to speculate who will be the losers—that is, the children.

KEY POINTS

1. Individual children should not be seen as bad—bad behavior is a manifestation of something that's wrong in a child's life.
2. It is helpful to think of children's lives as inextricably linked to the lives of parent's careers and siblings, so support the family to support the child.
3. Schools must be clear and explicit about what behavior in school is encouraged, what is acceptable and what is unacceptable, and how the penalties and rewards for such behaviors will be administered. A behavior policy should be publicized in every school and parents asked to sign up to it. A Pupil Charter should refer to behavior and children encouraged to sign up.
4. Teachers must involve children when devising the behavior policy. Their aspiration must be to build trust across the school community, teachers and teaching assistants, school managers, younger children to be supported by older children in respect to bullying and so forth, and students of all ages to be able to rely on one another and the school professionals.

NOTES

1. Kandel, I. (1933). Studies in Comparative Education, p.xix. (my italics).
2. Every Child Matters: Change for Children, www.everychildmatters.gov.uk.
3. Available at http://www.legislation.gov.uk/ukpga/2004/31/contents.
4. Bridie McDonagh, Senior Officer Children's Services, London Borough of Ealing Foreword to LBE's Behaviour Support Plan 2010.
5. The act is available at http://www.legislation.gov.uk/ukpga/2006/40/contents.
6. See http://dera.ioe.ac.uk/5680/1/633.pdf.
7. Exclusion means that children are sent home from school and banned from returning until certain conditions are met.
8. Because education in the United Kingdom is compulsory until the age of sixteen, parents who fail to ensure their children attend school regularly are breaking the law. If their children are truant persistently the parents risk being sent to prison.
9. The Department for Education (DfE), "Ensuring Good Behaviour in Schools: A Summary for Heads, Governing Bodies, Teachers, Parents and Pupils," 2011.
10. For a story on the report, see http://www.theguardian.com/education/2011/apr/28/pupil-behaviour-survey-schools.
11. The rankings used are Outstanding, Good, Satisfactory and Inadequate.
12. For many years children with learning difficulties of all kinds were educated in Special Schools. Research indicates that children with special educational needs (SEN) do much better when they are educated alongside children in a mainstream class. It is therefore policy to keep children in the mainstream wherever possible.
13. http://www.ofsted.gov.uk/resources/special-educational-needs-and-disability-towards-inclusive-schools.
14. DfE, *Permanent and Fixed Period Exclusions from Schools in England 2009/2010*, https://www.gov.uk/government/publications/permanent-and-fixed-period-exclusions-from-schools-in-england-academic-year-2009-to-2010.

15. National Strategies Inclusion—website cited in *Best Behaviour; School Discipline, Intervention and Exclusion.* London: Policy Exchange, 2011, p.11.

16. National Strategies Inclusion – website cited in *Best Behaviour; School Discipline, Intervention and Exclusion.* London: Policy Exchange, 2011, p.11.

17. FSM eligibility is seen as a powerful indicator of economic deprivation.

18. When a person uses a mobile phone or the internet to bully or harass another person.

19. TeachingTeachers' workloadSchoolsPupil behaviourguardian.co.uk, in Guardian Education, July 30, 2011.

20. Children's age or certain other factors may influence their ability to give informed consent.

21. This phrase is used to describe children who have been taken away from their parents and placed into the care of the LA for their own safety or welfare: they are placed either in residential homes for children or in foster care.

22. DfES Circular /0242/2002).

23. Ibid.

24. Ibid.

25. Ibid.

26. Interestingly the tawse, used in the north of England, comes from the Scots word for the plural of taw, for a leather strap sometimes with two tails.

27. Williams v Eady (1893) 10 T.L.R. 41.

28. National Union of Teachers (2009) NUT NOTES Education the Law and You, NUT, p. 3.

29. Available at http://www.legislation.gov.uk/ukpga/1989/41/contents.

30. See https://www.gov.uk.

31. Allegra Stratton, *The Guardian*, August 16, 2011.

32. See http://webarchive.nationalarchives.gov.uk/20130802140618/https:/www.education.gov.uk/aboutdfe/departmentalinformation/educationbill/a0073748/education-bill.

33. Available at https://www.gov.uk/government/publications/the-importance-of-teaching-the-schools-white-paper-2010

34. Inspection 2012 Proposals for inspection arrangements for maintained schools and academies from January 2012; For consultation, Ofsted.

Chapter Five

Disciplining Students in the United States

An Ongoing Challenge

Charles J. Russo

As reflected by the legal issues reviewed in the chapters in this volume, a continuing concern in the United States[1] and nations around the world is how to maintain safe and orderly learning environments for children and other members of educational communities while safeguarding the legal rights of students who are accused of violating disciplinary rules. Considering the explosion of litigation in the area of student rights over the better part of the last half century in the United States,[2] this chapter takes a focused approach to discipline in American public schools.[3]

In examining the status of student discipline in American public schools, an ongoing challenge for educators to be sure, this chapter is divided into four primary sections. The first part of the chapter provides an overview of the American legal system as the context in which disputes are resolved. Insofar as there is so much litigation on point, the second section of the chapter begins by focusing on student discipline generally before reviewing out of school conduct, zero tolerance policies, punishments (including corporal punishment as well as suspensions and expulsions), and due process hearings. The third part of the chapter briefly reviews the expansive and complicated topics of disciplining children with disabilities.[4]

Since they are overly expansive topics, this chapter does not deal with the voluminous litigation involving searches and seizures[5] or sexual harassment[6] even in recognizing that these issues typically involve student discipline and due process concerns; neither does this chapter deal with the free speech rights of students.[7] The fourth part of the chapter briefly addresses emerging issues in student discipline. The chapter ends with a brief conclusion.

THE AMERICAN LEGAL SYSTEM

The U.S. Constitution is the law of the land. In other words, the Constitution provides the framework within which the entire American legal system operates. Accordingly, actions of federal, state, and local governments including state constitutions, statutes, regulations, and common law, all of which impact the law of education as it pertains to disciplining students, are subject to the Constitution as interpreted by the Supreme Court and lower courts.

As important as education is, it is not mentioned in the U.S. Constitution. Under the Tenth Amendment, according to which "[t]he powers not delegated to the United States by the Constitution, nor prohibited by it to the States, are reserved to the States respectively, or to the people," then, education is primarily the concern of individual states.

Federal courts can intervene in educational disputes if a federal right is at issue such as in *Brown v. Board of Education (Brown)*.[8] In *Brown*, the Supreme Court struck down state-sanctioned racial segregation in public schools on the basis that officials violated students' rights to equal protection under the Fourteenth Amendment rather than on the right to education per se.

Along with identifying the rights of Americans, the Constitution establishes three coequal branches of government, all of which are involved in safeguarding the rights of students. The legislative, executive, and judicial branches of government give rise to the three other sources of law. The legislative branch "makes the law." Once bills complete the legislative process, they are signed into law by a chief executive such as a president or governor who has the power to enforce them through regulations written by personnel at administrative agencies.

The fourth and final source of law is judge-made or common law. Common law requires judges to "interpret the law,"[9] examining issues that may have been overlooked in the legislative or regulatory process or that may not have been anticipated when statutes were enacted. Common law involves the concept of precedent, the notion that a majority ruling of the highest court in a given jurisdiction is binding on lower courts within its jurisdiction. A ruling of the U.S. Supreme Court is thus binding throughout the nation, while decisions of state supreme court are binding only in given jurisdictions.

The federal judiciary and most state court systems consist of three levels: trial courts, intermediate appellate courts, and courts of last resort. In the federal system, trial courts are known as federal district courts; state trial courts use a variety of names. Each state has at least one federal district court while densely populated states, such as California and New York, have as many as four.

Trial courts typically involve a judge and a jury. The role of the judge, as trier of law, is to apply the law by deciding, for instance, whether evidence is admissible while providing direction for juries on how to apply the law to the facts of the specific cases that they are examining. There are thirteen federal intermediate appellate courts known as Circuit Courts of Appeal; state intermediate appellate courts employ a variety of names. The highest court in the United States is the Supreme Court; although most states refer to their high courts as supreme courts, a variety of titles are in use.

DISCIPLINE GENERALLY

Recognizing the increasingly difficult challenge facing educational officials, courts grant them "wide discretion in school discipline matters"[10] to ensure safe and orderly learning environments by adopting reasonable policies and procedures regulating student conduct. Of course, whether rules are enforceable depends on fact-specific analysis of disputes during litigation.

Whether all rules are written is often inconsequential where offenses such as not turning in homework assignments, cheating, and talking either during class or out of turn are punishable under general expectations in schools. Insofar as courts concede that educators cannot develop written rules for all possible student rule violations, they typically defer to the authority of educators as long as they impose discipline that meets the requirements of due process.

When students know,[11] or reasonably ought to know, school rules and the punishments applied by educators are appropriate to their offenses,[12] such as getting a zero for cheating on an examination, regardless of whether misbehavior occurs in schools or away from schools, courts are unlikely to interfere as long as officials treat similarly situated individuals similarly by providing them with the required level of due process.[13] While students certainly have a right to know what conduct is prohibited, school rules need not meet the same standard that courts apply in criminal cases which calls for a higher burden of proof in establishing guilt or innocence.[14]

Out-of-School Conduct

The authority of school officials to discipline students for their off-campus misconduct has led to a large amount of litigation with most courts deferring to educators as long as rules satisfy due process. Clearly, educators can regulate student conduct that violates school rules even if it occurs at extracurricular activities such as football games.[15] It is, though, more difficult to enforce conduct rules outside of school due to potential conflicts with the rights of parents and attenuated connections between student behavior and the educational process. As discussed briefly below as an emerging topic, courts reach mixed results in this emerging area of student use of the internet outside of schools such as in their own homes.

Putting aside cases involving search and seizure under the Fourth Amendment to the U.S. Constitution and similar provisions in state constitutions, a topic beyond the scope of this chapter, courts typically refuse to intervene in disputes where rules prevent drug use and/or alcohol consumption. Courts tend to not get involved in these disputes regardless of whether infractions occur on campus, especially by student-athletes, but not exclusively limited to them, for two reasons.

First, insofar it is well-settled that participating in extracurricular activities, whether such organizations as the National Honor Society[16] or sports,[17] is a privilege rather than a right, educators can impose higher disciplinary standards on students who participate in these activities. Second, officials can base rules on health and safety concerns. In either circumstance, educators can suspend or dismiss students who violate team or activity rules regardless of whether parents approve of the behavior of their children.

At the same time, rules cannot be too broad such as where one forbade student-athletes from being in cars where beer was being transported.[18] Yet, presence at events where alcohol is being consumed can provide the justification for rendering student-athletes ineligible[19] as can drinking alcohol at school-sponsored events.[20] Moreover, rules must be applied equally to males and females[21] when officials dismiss players from teams.

As to punishments, a federal trial court in Wisconsin reiterated the legal principle that educational officials must rely on sufficient evidence and fair processes when disciplining students.[22] Courts agree that students can be punished for off-campus activities that threaten the health or safety of those in school such as off-campus misbehaviors as drug sales,[23] possession of tobacco[24] or drugs,[25] and committing aggravated assaults[26] on school sponsored trips.

Zero-Tolerance Policies

As a subset of issues surrounding misbehavior typically associated with student substance abuse and violence, whether in or around schools, many boards adopted zero-tolerance policies in attempts to remedy, if not eliminate problems with regard to drugs, alcohol, tobacco, and weapons. Insofar as such policies tend to deny educators discretion in making decisions, courts have reached mixed results when they are challenged. When reviewing zero-tolerance policies, usually courts look to ensure that school officials acted with discretion in disciplining students.

When applying zero-tolerance policies, courts reached mixed results as to students who possessed knives in schools. For example, when school officials in Tennessee discovered a hunting knife in the glove compartment of a student's car, but it did not belong to him, the Sixth Circuit ruled that his proposed expulsion for possession of a weapon, pursuant to a zero-tolerance policy under which students could have been disciplined for not knowingly possessing weapons, was invalid because it was not rationally related to a legitimate state interest.[27]

Conversely, the Fourth Circuit affirmed that educators could suspend a student who had a knife in his locker even though he took it from a suicidal schoolmate.[28] The court was satisfied that officials provided the student with due process before he was suspended.

In Florida, an appellate court refused to intervene on behalf of a student who was suspended for bringing a gun to school under a zero-tolerance policy.[29] The court dismissed the claim insofar as it lacked jurisdiction under state law. Earlier, the federal trial court in South Dakota upheld a student's being disciplined for violating her school's zero-tolerance policy by using profanity.[30]

PUNISHMENTS

Generally

As discussed earlier, courts realize that educators need to use their discretion when disciplining students who break school rules.[31] If disciplinary rules and procedures satisfy due process as fundamentally fair, courts usually uphold the actions of educators as long as they are not arbitrary, capricious, or unreasonable.

Many of the cases discussed in this chapter demonstrate that courts have long taken the sex, age, and size as well as the mental, emotional, and physical conditions of students and the nature of their offenses into consideration when reviewing penalties.[32] For instance, when a student received a ten-day suspension for using inappropriate and disrespectful language to educators, a federal trial court in Michigan rejected his claim that they violated his rights to due process because he missed his graduation ceremony and other senior events.[33] The court reasoned that insofar as the student received all of the process he was due and the punishment was rationally related to his offense, his claim was without merit.

As noted, courts ordinarily do not review student conduct rules with the same scrutiny as they use in criminal cases. In *Wood v. Strickland*, involving the attempted expulsion of students in Arkansas for consuming alcoholic beverages at school or school-sponsored activities, the Supreme Court acknowledged as much. The court pointed out that the federal judiciary is not supposed to "supplant the interpretation of [a] regulation of those officers who adopted it and are entrusted with its enforcement."[34]

Among the many cases dealing with punishments, courts refused to overturn such penalties as receiving a grade of zero for the first offense of plagiarism on an assignment;[35] being expelled for bringing a weapon to school;[36] being named a ward of the court for bringing a knife to school;[37] being dismissed from a marching band for missing a performance;[38] being seated at an isolated desk due to disruptive behavior;[39] and being suspended for turning in an assignment which expressed the desire to blow up the school.[40] Moreover, courts have upheld adjudications of juvenile delinquency against students for making obscene remarks to a teacher;[41] threatening a teacher;[42] being disruptive at school;[43] bringing a plastic toy gun to school;[44] making a false fire alarm report at school;[45] violating a law against the possession of a weapon at school by bringing a paintball gun and markers to school;[46] and threatening to blow a counselor's brains out with a shotgun.[47]

Other courts invalidated a variety of sanctions as too harsh. Courts overturned such penalties as a conviction for disorderly conduct where a student threatened to shoot up a school since no one took him seriously and there were no weapons in his home;[48] assault for throwing a partially eaten apple at a teacher;[49] adjudication as a juvenile delinquent for having a butter knife in a locker since it was incapable of being used as a deadly weapon;[50] and repeatedly using insulting and vulgar language to address a teacher.[51]

Corporal Punishment

According to the common law, teachers have the right to administer reasonable corporal punishment. In fact, absent growing statutory prohibitions against corporal punishment[52] rendering it illegal in more than half of the states, educators may employ the practice even against parental wishes[53] as long as local board policies authorize its use.[54]

Unless they are contrary to state law, local board policies with regard to the imposition of corporal punishment are generally controlling.[55] The use of unreasonable corporal punishment, a determination that is ultimately a question of fact for a jury to resolve, or behavior violating board policy or state law has served as the cause for dismissing teachers.[56]

In its only case on the merits of the practice, *Ingraham v. Wright,*[57] the Supreme Court refused to treat corporal punishment as unconstitutional in all circumstances. It ruled that the Eighth Amendment's prohibition against cruel and unusual punishments was designed to protect those guilty of crimes and was inapplicable to paddling students in order to preserve discipline, not protect children. Noting that most jurisdictions at that time permitted its use, and that professional and public opinion was divided on the practice, the court refused to strike down corporal punishment as unconstitutional.

Turning to fact-specific cases, the Fourth,[58] Tenth,[59] and Eleventh[60] Circuits, as well as federal trial courts,[61] agreed that students can proceed with substantive due process claims where punishments are "so brutal, demeaning, and harmful as literally to shock the conscience of a court."[62] In such a case, the Fourth Circuit affirmed the denial of a wrestling coach's claim for qualified immunity where a student sued him and other school officials after the coach encouraged members of his team to beat the plaintiff repeatedly.[63]

In two other cases, though, the Fifth Circuit disagreed, explaining that state statutory and common law provisions offered better redress as to damages and possible criminal liability rather than vitiate the use of corporal punishment.[64] Most litigation involving corporal punishment has been resolved in favor of teachers based on the presumption of correctness which complaining students and parents were unable to overcome.[65]

Suspension and Expulsion

Suspension and expulsion are the most serious penalties that school officials can impose on students. Suspensions generally refer to temporary exclusions for set periods or until students satisfy specific conditions while expulsions are permanent removals from school. On a related point, whether students are entitled to educational services during expulsions varies from one jurisdiction to the next. The elements of due process depend to a significant extent on the length of the exclusions under consideration.

Due Process and Punishments

Courts generally defer to educators who use reasonable forms of discipline and can justify their actions.[66] Cases often hinge on whether officials provided students with adequate procedural due process. While due process does not require educators to afford students all of the safeguards present in criminal,[67] or, for that matter, civil,[68] proceedings, essential elements depend on the circumstances and seriousness of potential punishments. At the very least, students who are subject to significant disciplinary penalties are entitled to notice and opportunities to respond in the presence of fair and impartial third-party decision makers.[69]

The Fifth Circuit provided the earliest guidelines, admittedly from a dispute in higher education, as to required notice and hearings prior to long-term exclusions where a student faced expulsion from a public college for non-academic reasons.[70] The court reasoned that notice should contain a statement of the specific charges and grounds which, if proven, would justify an expulsion. The court also decided that insofar as assessing misconduct depends on gathering facts that can be easily colored by witnesses, a fair and impartial third-party decision maker must hear both sides in considerable detail.

Expressly rejecting the requirement of "a full-dress judicial hearing, with the right to cross-examine witnesses,"[71] the Fifth Circuit observed that "the rudiments of an adversary proceeding . . . [require that] . . . student[s] should be given the names of the witnesses against him and an oral or written report on the facts to which each witness testifies. [They] should also be given the opportunity to present . . . [their] own defense against the charges and to produce either oral testimony or written affidavits of witnesses in [their] behalf."[72]

In *Goss v. Lopez* (*Goss*),[73] arguably the high water mark of student rights, the Supreme Court set out the minimum constitutional requirements when dealing with suspensions of ten days or less. In a dispute from Ohio, students who did not receive a hearing challenged their suspensions for allegedly disruptive conduct.

Ruling in favor of the students, the *Goss* Supreme Court mandated that due process requires that they be given "oral or written notice of the charges against [them] and, if [they] den[y] them, an explanation of the evidence the authorities have and an opportunity to present [their] side of the story."[74] The court held that there is no need for a delay between when officials give students notice and the time of their hearings, conceding that in most cases disciplinarians may well have informally discussed alleged acts of misconduct with them shortly after they occurred.[75]

The *Goss* court pointed out that if the presence of students constitutes threats of disruption, they may be removed immediately with the due process requirements to be fulfilled as soon as practicable. The court expressly rejected the notion that students should be represented by counsel, be able to present witnesses, and be able to confront and cross-examine witnesses when facing short-term exclusions.[76]

In its analysis, the Supreme Court added that "[l]onger suspensions or expulsions for the remainder of the school term, or permanently, may require more formal procedures . . . [and that] in unusual situations, although involving only a short suspension, something more than the rudimentary procedures will be required."[77] States have followed the court's suggestion by developing statutory guidelines when students are subject to long-term suspensions or expulsions.

Following *Goss*, federal trial courts began to apply its procedural requirements to student disciplinary transfers[78] and three-day suspensions.[79] The courts agreed that where the property interests of students were involved, they were of sufficient magnitude to qualify for the minimal constitutional due process protections. A federal trial court in Texas reached the same result where a student received a three-day suspension for taking allegedly compromising photographs of the principal's car while it was parked in front of a female teacher's house.[80] The Fifth Circuit later upheld a student's suspension for less than ten days, agreeing that officials did not violate his rights to due process in light of his role in an attack on his school's computer network.[81]

In cases involving criminal misconduct, the Fifth[82] and Eleventh[83] Circuits was satisfied that insofar as students who were transferred to alternative schools within their districts did not suffer the losses of property interests, they lacked rights to hearings. On the other hand, the Sixth Circuit remanded a dispute where a student was transferred due to criminal misbehavior for consideration of whether the failure of officials to afford him a hearing violated his rights to due process.[84]

The argument that more extensive processes are necessary if disciplinary penalties indirectly lead to academic sanctions has led to mixed judicial results. The Seventh Circuit refused to intervene where a student's three-day suspension for drinking alcohol in violation of school rules delayed his graduation.[85]

Courts disagree as to the precise requirements of procedural due process in connection with penalties that are more severe than the ten-day suspension involved in *Goss*. The bottom line is that educators must act with fairness. As such, most jurisdictions rely on the Supreme Court's perspective as set forth in *Mathews v. Eldridge*, that "[d]ue process is flexible and calls for such procedural protections as the particular situation demands."[86]

In such a case, where a student in Georgia was suspended for nine days for fighting, screaming obscenities, and refusing to cooperate with and assaulting faculty members in connection with her possession of look-alike drugs at school, the Eleventh Circuit affirmed that educators met the requirements of due process when her mother participated in a telephone call with them on the day that the incident occurred.[87]

Due Process Hearings

Courts do not expect students who are accused of school disciplinary infractions to receive full judicial proceedings.[88] Even so, courts agree that students facing expulsions are entitled to notice informing them of the time and place of some form of hearings.[89] At the same time, school officials should inform students of the charges and the nature of the evidence that they face[90] but not necessarily to prehearing notice of particular infractions.

In representative litigation, courts upheld expulsions where one student and his parents received repeated warnings that he faced expulsion for possession of marijuana[91] and another was arrested and charged with two counts of illegal sales of controlled substances.[92] Both courts agreed that the students were expelled after hearings that were presided over by fair and impartial third-party decision makers who based their actions on the contents of the records.[93]

Other courts decided that students are not entitled to have their own attorneys present as trial counsel[94] or at public expense if they can obtain pro bono lawyers,[95] or to know the identity of[96] and/or to confront witnesses,[97] especially if there may be clear and serious danger to student witnesses.[98]

A dispute arose where a state statute afforded students and their parents due process rights including notice, an opportunity to respond, the right to be represented by counsel, as well as to present evidence and question witnesses during their expulsion proceedings. When the student and his parents chose neither to have an attorney present during his initial hearing nor to exercise his statutory right to present evidence or question witnesses, the Supreme Court of South Carolina rejected their claim that officials violated his rights to procedural due process.[99]

As reflected by a case from the Sixth Circuit, there is a balance between the rights of students who are accused of wrongdoing to confront witnesses and the danger to accusers. The court conceded that the necessity of protecting student witnesses from reprisal and ostracism generally outweighs the value to the truth-seeking process of allowing them to cross-examine their accusers.[100] In addition, hearsay evidence used in hearings has withstood judicial scrutiny when allowing police or school officials to testify instead of protected student witnesses.[101]

Other courts agreed that students lack rights to hearing officers who are not school employees[102] or, as noted, to *Miranda* warnings when questioned by educational officials. Conversely, "although '[a]s a general matter, there is no hard and fast federal Constitutional right to call or cross-examine witnesses in a school disciplinary setting,'"[103] some courts granted students the right to cross-examine witnesses;[104] to have an attorney present;[105] to the presence of an impartial, non-school, third-party decision maker;[106] and to obtain a redacted copy of disciplinary records.[107]

In a case addressing aspects of due process, the Eighth Circuit affirmed that a middle school student in Arkansas failed to prove that educators violated his procedural due process rights when he was expelled as a result of an altercation with a teacher and principal. The court found that officials did not violate the student's rights because they fully informed his mother of the grounds for his expulsion and he received a hearing at which he was represented by counsel who had a full opportunity to examine and cross-examine witnesses.[108] The court pointed out that even though educators violated board rules by not supplying the student's attorney with the remarks of two witnesses in advance of the hearing, this was not a constitutional violation.[109]

According to an older federal case from Illinois, students facing long-term suspensions or expulsions did not have a right to stenographic or mechanical recordings of proceedings.[110] Almost thirty years later, another appellate court in Illinois denied a student's request for a verbatim transcript of his expulsion hearing.[111]

Similarly, the federal trial court in Massachusetts agreed that a student who was excluded from school for disruptive behavior was not entitled to a stenographic or mechanical recording of his expulsion hearing.[112] However, almost twenty years later, the Supreme Judicial Court of Massachusetts affirmed that when students ask that testimony given at closed hearings be recorded electronically, it must be honored.[113]

Challenges to disciplinary actions often involve disputes over whether school officials fully complied with statutory provisions or board policies. If infractions are minor and officials have not violated student rights, courts tend not to overturn the punishments. For instance, where a student did not receive the necessary written notice, but knew of the rules and charges, the Supreme Court of Vermont refused to invalidate his expulsion.[114]

Earlier, where a student in Mississippi admitted that he brought a switchblade to school in violation of board policy, the Fifth Circuit affirmed that it was unnecessary for all witnesses and their testimony to have been identified before the hearing.[115] Additionally, although officials in Minnesota may not have provided a precise rationale for a contemplated three-day suspension of students who distributed an unofficial newspaper in school containing vulgarity, but the evidence against them was so overwhelming that a second hearing would not have altered the outcome, the Eighth Circuit acknowledged that officials did not violate their rights to due process.[116]

DISCIPLINING STUDENTS WITH DISABILITIES

Following multiple earlier cases in a variety of jurisdictions, *Honig v. Doe* (*Honig*)[117] remains the Supreme Court's only case involving disciplining students with disabilities. In a dispute over whether educators in California could exclude two students with disabilities from school, the Justices affirmed that the stay-put provision in the Individuals with Disabilities Education Act[118] prohibits educators from unilaterally excluding students with disabilities from school for dangerous or disruptive actions that are manifestations of their disabilities during the pendency of review proceedings.

In Honig, the Supreme Court added that officials could impose normal, non-placement-changing procedures such as, "the use of study carrels, timeouts, detention, or the restriction of privileges,"[119] including temporary suspensions for up to ten school days, for students who posed immediate threats to school safety.

Unfortunately, *Honig* failed to resolve all of the legal issues surrounding how educators can discipline students with disabilities. Consequently, Congress sought to clarify the rights of students with disabilities as part of the

IDEA's 1997 Amendments.[120] These changes granted educators the authority to suspend special education students for not more than ten school days as long as the same kinds of sanctions apply to children who are not disabled.[121]

According to the IDEA's regulations, a series of removals resulting in a pattern of exclusions cumulatively having children with disabilities out of school for more than ten school days may be considered changes in placements.[122] The regulations make it clear that if students are suspended for misbehavior substantially similar to past actions that have been identified as manifestations of their disabilities, then this constitutes changes in placements.[123] In making such judgments, the regulations direct educators to consider the length of each removal, the total amount of time that children have been out of school, and the proximity of the removals to one another in evaluating whether changes in placements occurred.[124]

School officials can remove students with disabilities from school for separate, but dissimilar, acts of misconduct for more than ten cumulative days in school years.[125] After students with disabilities are removed from school for ten days in the same school year, during any later removals, educators must provide them with educational services.[126]

Under the 2004 amendments to the IDEA, educators have increased authority when dealing with students with disabilities who possess weapons or drugs at school.[127] Pursuant to an expanded definition of a dangerous weapon, the IDEA incorporates language from another federal statute such that it now includes instruments, devices, materials, and substances capable of inflicting harm in addition to firearms, but does not include small pocket knives.[128]

The IDEA defines illegal drugs as controlled substances but excludes those that may be legally prescribed by physicians.[129] Educators may thus transfer students with disabilities unilaterally to interim alternative placements for up to forty-five school days for carrying or possessing weapons[130] or for knowing possession, use, sale, or solicitation of drugs[131] on school property or at school functions as long as this sanction applies under like circumstances for peers who are not disabled.[132]

Another change in the 2004 version of the IDEA permits educators to place students who inflicted serious bodily injury on others at school, on school premises, or at school functions in alternative educational settings.[133] In explicating "serious bodily injury," the IDEA relies on another federal statute which defines the term as involving a substantial risk of death, extreme physical pain, protracted and obvious disfigurement, or protracted loss or impairment of the function of a bodily member, organ, or mental faculty.[134]

Under the IDEA's interim alternative placement provisions, educators must allow students to continue to progress in general curricula where they still receive necessary services outlined in their IEPs.[135] Further, school officials must provide students with services and modifications designed to prevent the misbehaviors from recurring.[136]

When students are moved to alternative placements for more than ten school days,[137] educators must conduct functional behavioral assessments (FBAs) and implement behavioral intervention plans (BIPs) if they are not already in place.[138] If plans were in place when children misbehaved, IEP teams must review them and their implementation in order to make any necessary modifications.[139] If parents disagree with alternative placements and request hearings, consistent with the IDEA's stay-put provision, children must remain in their alternative settings.[140] On the expiration of the forty-five day periods, educators must return students to their former settings even if hearings on school board proposals to change their placements are pending unless parents and educators agree otherwise.[141]

Educators must complete FBAs and BIPs if they view disciplinary infractions as manifestations of students' disabilities.[142] As important as FBAs and BIPs can be, though, and as directive as the IDEA and its regulations are, neither addresses their content or form. Moreover, there is little case law addressing this issue.[143]

The IDEA includes definitions and procedures to evaluate whether, on "case-by-case determinations,"[144] misconduct is related to students' disabilities.[145] The IDEA defines a manifestation as conduct caused by or having a direct and substantial relationship to students' disabilities or as the direct result of the failure of school officials to implement IEPs properly. In reviewing whether placements are inappropriate, key members of IEP teams should gather and use the same standards they worked with in prospectively evaluating whether proposed placements were appropriate.[146]

If teams interpret misconduct as either manifestations of students' disabilities or as results of improperly implemented IEPs, children may not be expelled or suspended for more than ten days and school officials must reconsider their current placements.[147] In rendering manifestation determinations, teams must consider all relevant information, including evaluations and diagnostic results as well as student observations.[148]

As with other aspects related to special education, manifestation determinations are subject to the IDEA's administrative appeals process. The IDEA now directs school officials to expedite hearings incident to manifestation determinations. Hearings must occur within twenty school days of the dates on which they were requested and hearing officers must render decisions within ten days of hearings.[149]

If parents contest the outcomes of manifestation determinations, educators must delay long-term suspensions or expulsions until hearings are completed while students may remain in interim alternative educational settings.[150] Along with retaining students in their then current, or pendent, placements, hearing officers may issue change in placement orders.[151]

Language in the revised IDEA addresses whether school officials can discontinue services for children who are properly expelled for misconduct that is not related to their disabilities. In codifying a federal policy directing officials to provide services for a student who was excluded for misbehavior unrelated to his disability, the IDEA essentially repudiated earlier litigation which rejected the position that such a requirement existed. [152]

The IDEA requires boards to provide appropriate educational placements for all students with disabilities including those who have been expelled from school. [153] As a result, even if students are expelled for disciplinary infractions unrelated to their disabilities, they must be provided with services allowing them to progress toward achieving their IEP goals. [154]

In resolving disputes over the status of students who were not yet assessed for special education but claimed to have been covered by the IDEA officials must now provide the law's protections to individuals if they knew that children were disabled before they misbehaved. [155] Educators may be considered to be on notice in light of students' prior behavioral and academic performances and the concerns of teachers about their performances. [156] An exception exists if educators already conducted evaluations and concluded that students were not disabled or if parents refused to grant their permission for evaluations or declined offered special education services. [157]

If parents request evaluations when students are subject to disciplinary sanctions, they must be conducted in an expedited manner. [158] Consistent with the IDEA's stay-put provision, until expedited evaluations are completed, students must remain in the placements deemed appropriate by educators. [159] If evaluation teams have reason to believe that children are disabled, they must provide students with special education services. [160]

The IDEA's discipline provisions allow school officials to report crimes committed by students to the proper authorities or impeding law enforcement and judicial authorities from carrying out their duties. [161] If officials report crimes, they must make copies of students' special education and disciplinary records available to appropriate authorities. [162]

EMERGING ISSUES

As in other parts of the world, courts and educational leaders have difficulty keeping pace with technological advancements particularly as they impact student expressive activities in and around schools. This interplay between student rights to free speech and the ability of educators to ensure safe and orderly learning environments, presents perhaps the greatest challenge for school officials in the United States as they who seek to look after the well-being of all of the students in their care. [163]

Coupled with the fact that many of the cases involving cyber-bullying, whether of peers [164] or teachers, [165] and that inappropriate websites were often created in private homes rather than schools raises novel questions about the authority of educators to intervene. These cases have led to seemingly paradoxical outcomes as students [166] have prevailed in some litigation while school officials [167] have triumphed in other cases. It should be interesting to observe how this issue plays itself out in coming years.

CONCLUSION

Clearly, one of the greatest challenges facing educational leaders and teachers is devising school rules that help to create safe and orderly learning environments. By reviewing the litigation and issues described in this chapter, hopefully educators can devise systems of discipline that respect the rights of all members of school communities.

KEY POINTS

1. Students have varying rights to due process when subjected to discipline in American public schools.
2. For minor infractions where students knew, or should have known the law, school officials can act unilaterally as long as punishments are appropriate to the offenses.
3. Students are entitled to due process hearings when they will be out of school for ten days or longer.
4. Disciplining students with disabilities is a complex process. If the misbehavior is related to students' disabilities, educational officials must provide significant procedural due process if they are to be removed from their current placements for ten days or more.

NOTES

1. This chapter relies in part on material covered in chapter 13, on student rights, in Charles J. Russo, *Reutter's The Law of Public Education*, 8th ed. (New York, NY: Foundation Press, 2012).

2. Recognizing that multiple suits can be used for most of the issues discussed in this chapter, the footnotes cite to leading representative disputes rather than provide exhaustive lists of cases.

3. Insofar as student behaviors are largely matters of contract based on the fact that their parents paid to have them attend non-public schools, disputes from these schools are beyond the scope of this chapter.

4. For more detail on this topic, see Allan G. Osborn and Charles J. Russo, *Procedural Requirements for Disciplining Students with Disabilities* (Cleveland, OH: Education Law Association, 2014).

5. For a comprehensive review of Fourth Amendment issues, see Charles J. and Ralph D. Mawdsley, *Searches, Seizures and Drug Testing Procedures: Balancing Rights and School Safety*, 2nd ed. (Sarasota, FL: LRP Publications, 2012); (3rd ed. currently in preparation).

6. See Charles J. Russo, "A Legal Primer on Sexual Harassment: Lessons for Practice from the United States." *Australia and New Zealand Journal of Law and Education* 13(1) (2008): 21–48.

7. See Allan G. Osborne and Charles J. Russo, "Can Students Be Disciplined for Off-campus Cyberspeech: The Reach of the First Amendment in the Age of Technology." *Brigham Young University Education and Law Journal* 2012 (2012): 331–67.

8. 347 U.S. 483 (1954).

9. For an article on the judicial process, see Charles J. Russo, "Judges as Umpires or Rule Makers? The Role of the Judiciary in Educational Decision Making in the United States." *Education Law Journal* 10(1) (2009): 33–47.

10. *DMP v. Fay Sch. ex rel. Bd. of Trustees*, 933 F. Supp.2d 214, 222 (D. Mass. 2013) (internal citations omitted).

11. *Martinez v. School Dist. No. 60*, 852 P.2d 1275 (Colo. Ct. App. 1992).

12. *Kolesnick By and Through Shaw v. Omaha Pub. Sch. Dist.*, 558 N.W.2d 807 (Neb. 1997).

13. *Goss v. Lopez*, 419 U.S. 565 (1975).

14. *Wiemerslage Through Wiemerslage v. Maine Twp. High Sch. Dist. 207*, 29 F.3d 1149 (7th Cir. 1994).

15. *Fuller ex rel. Fuller v. Decatur Pub. Sch. Bd. of Educ. School Dist. 61*, 251 F.3d 662 (7th Cir. 2001).

16. *Piekosz-Murphy v. Board of Educ. of Cmty. High Sch. Dist. No. 230*, 858 F. Supp.2d 952 (N.D. Ill. 2012).

17. *Lowery v. Euverard*, 497 F.3d 584 (6th Cir. 2007), *cert. denied*, 555 U.S. 825, (2008); *Palmer v. Merluzzi*, 868 F.2d 90 (3d Cir. 1989); *Braesch v. DePasquale*, 265 N.W.2d 842 (Neb. 1978), *cert. denied*, 439 U.S. 1068 (1979).

18. *Bunger v. Iowa High Sch. Athletic Ass'n*, 197 N.W.2d 555 (Iowa 1972).

19. *Bush v. Dassel–Cokato Bd. of Educ.*, 745 F. Supp. 562 (D. Minn. 1990).

20. *Katchak v. Glasgow Indep. Sch. Sys.*, 690 F. Supp. 580 (W.D. Ky. 1988).

21. *Schultzen v. Woodbury Cent. Cmty. Sch. Dist.*, 187 F. Supp.2d 1099 (N.D. Iowa 2002) (holding that a female student-athlete could not be punished more harshly than males for the same offense of smoking in violation of athletic training rules).

22. *Butler v. Oak Creek–Franklin Sch. Dist.*, 172 F. Supp.2d 1102 (E.D. Wis. 2001).

23. *Howard v. Colonial Sch. Dist.*, 621 A.2d 362 (Del. Super. Ct. 1992), *aff'd without published opinion*, 615 A.2d 531 (Del. 1992).

24. *Ette ex rel. Ette v. Linn–Mar Cmty. Sch. Dist.*, 656 N.W.2d 62 (Iowa 2002) (sending an eighth grader home from a band trip for possessing cigarettes).

25. *Rhodes v. Guarricino*, 54 F. Supp.2d 186 (S.D.N.Y. 1999).

26. *Pollnow v. Glennon*, 757 F.2d 496 (2d Cir. 1985).

27. *Seal v. Morgan*, 229 F.3d 567 (6th Cir. 2000).

28. *Ratner v. Loudoun Cnty. Pub. Schs.*, 16 Fed.Appx. 140 (4th Cir. 2001), *cert. denied*, 534 U.S. 1114 (2002).

29. *D.K. ex rel. Kennedy v. District Sch. Bd. Indian River Cnty.*, 981 So. 2d 667 (Fla. Dist. Ct. App. 2008).

30. *Anderson v. Milbank Sch. Dist. 25–4*, 197 F.R.D. 682 (D.S.D. 2000).

31. *Spacek v. Charles*, 928 S.W.2d 88 (Tex. Ct. App. 1996).

32. See, for example, *Berry v. Arnold Sch. Dist.*, 137 S.W.2d 256 (Ark. 1940).

33. *Posthumus v. Board of Educ. of Mona Shores Pub. Schs.*, 380 F. Supp.2d 891 (W.D. Mich. 2005).

34. 420 U.S. 308 (1975), *reh'g denied*, 421 U.S. 921 (1975), *on remand sub nom. Strickland v. Inlow*, 519 F.2d 744 (8th Cir. 1975).

35. *Zellman ex rel. M.Z. v. Independent Sch. Dist. No. 2758*, 594 N.W.2d 216 (Minn. Ct. App. 1999).

36. *J.M. v. Webster Cnty. Bd. of Educ.*, 534 S.E.2d 50 (W. Va. 2000).

37. *In re Randy G.*, 110 Cal.Rptr.2d 516 (Cal. 2001).

38. *Mazevski v. Horseheads Cent. Sch. Dist.*, 950 F. Supp.69 (W.D.N.Y. 1997).

39. *Cole by Cole v. Greenfield–Cent. Cmty. Schs.*, 657 F. Supp. 56 (S.D. Ind. 1986).

40. *Cuff ex rel. B.C. v. Valley Cent. Sch. Dist.*, 714 F. Supp2d 462 (S.D.N.Y. 2010).

41. *In Interest of D.A.D.*, 481 S.E.2d 262 (Ga. Ct. App. 1997).

42. *In re J.H.*, 797 A.2d 260 (Pa. Super. Ct. 2002).

43. *In re D.H.* 663 S.E.2d 139 (Ga. 2008); *M.C. v. State*, 695 So. 2d 477 (Fla. Dist. Ct. App.1997), *review denied*, 700 So. 2d 686 (Fla. 1997).

44. *In re B.N.S.*, 641 S.E.2d 411 (N.C. Ct. App. 2007).

45. *In re C.R.K.*, 56 S.W.3d 288 (Tex. Ct. App. 2001).

46. *In re M.H.M.*, 864 A.2d 1251 (Pa. Super. Ct. 2004), *appeal denied*, 880 A.2d 1239 (Pa. 2005).

47. *Andrews v. State*, 930 A.2d 846 (Del. 2007).

48. *State v. McCooey*, 802 A.2d 1216 (N.H. 2002).

49. *In re Gavin T.*, 77 Cal.Rptr.2d 701 (Cal. Ct. App. 1998).

50. *In re Melanie H.*, 706 A.2d 621 (Md. Ct. App. 1998).

51. *In re Nickolas S.*, 245 P.3d 446 (Ariz. 2011).

52. See, for example, Cal. Educ. Code § 49000; Iowa Code Ann. § 280.21; Mich. Comp. Laws Ann. § 380.1312; Neb. Rev. Stat. Ann. § 79–295, N.D. Cent. Code 15.1–19–02 Utah Code Ann. § 53A–11–802; Va. Code Ann. § 22.1–279.1; Wash. Rev. Code Ann. § 28A.150.300; W. Va. Code Ann. § 18A–5–1; Wis. Stat. Ann. § 118.31

53. *Baker v. Owen*, 395 F. Supp. 294 (M.D.N.C. 1975), *aff'd*, 423 U.S. 907 (1975) (agreeing that parental disapproval of corporal punishment did not preclude its use on a child).

54. *Ware v. Estes*, 328 F. Supp. 657 (N.D. Tex. 1971), *aff'd*, 458 F.2d 1360 (5th Cir. 1972), *cert. denied*, 409 U.S. 1027 (1972).

55. *McKinney v. Greene*, 379 So. 2d 69 (La. Ct. App. 1979), *writ denied*, 379 So. 2d 69 (La. Ct. App. 1979).

56. See, for example, *McPherson v. New York City Dep't of Educ.*, 457 F.3d 211 (2d Cir. 2006); *Bott v. Board of Educ., Deposit Cent. Sch. Dist.*, 392 N.Y.S.2d 274 (N.Y. 1977).

57. 430 U.S. 651 (1977).

58. *Hall v. Tawney*, 621 F.2d 607 (4th Cir. 1980).

59. *Garcia v. Miera*, 817 F.2d 650 (10th Cir. 1987), *cert. denied*, 485 U.S. 959 (1988).

60. *Neal v. Fulton Cnty. Bd. of Educ.*, 229 F.3d 1069 (11th Cir. 2000), *reh'g en banc denied*, 244 F.3d 143 (11th Cir. 2000).

61. See, for example, *Nicol v. Auburn–Washburn USD 437*, 231 F. Supp.2d 1107 (D. Kan. 2002).

62. *Hall v. Tawney*, 621 F.2d 607, 613 (4th Cir. 1980).

63. *Meeker v. Edmundson*, 415 F.3d 317 (4th Cir. 2005).

64. *Cunningham v. Beavers*, 858 F.2d 269 (5th Cir. 1988), *cert. denied*, 489 U.S. 1067 (1989); *Moore v. Willis Indep. Sch. Dist.*, 233 F.3d 871 (5th Cir. 2000), *reh'g en banc denied*, 248 F.3d 1145 (5th Cir. 2001).

65. See also *Fox v. Cleveland*, 169 F. Supp.2d 977 (W.D. Ark. 2001); *Campbell v. Gahanna–Jefferson Bd. of Educ.*, 717 N.E.2d 347 (Ohio Ct. App. 1998); *Burnham v. Stevens*, 734 So. 2d 256 (Miss. Ct. App. 1999).

66. See *In re Expulsion of N.Y.B.*, 750 N.W.2d 318 (Minn. Ct. App. 2008) (remanding a board's expulsion of a student for a calendar year for further consideration where it was unclear whether officials provided sufficient detail justifying their action).

67. See, for example, *Brewer by Dreyfus v. Austin Indep. Sch. Dist.*, 779 F.2d 260 (5th Cir. 1985).

68. *Colquitt v. Rich Twp. High Sch. Dist. No. 227*, 699 N.E.2d 1109 (Ill. App. Ct. 1998).

69. See, for example, *G.C. v. Owensboro Pub. Schs.*, 711 F.3d 623 (6th Cir. 2013); *Wynar v. Douglas Cnty. Sch. Dist.*, 728 F.3d 1062 (9th Cir. 2013).

70. *Dixon v. Alabama State Bd. of Educ.*, 294 F.2d 150 (5th Cir. 1961), *cert. denied*, 368 U.S. 930 (1961).

71. *Id.* at 159.

72. *Id.*

73. 419 U.S. 565 (1975).

74. *Id.* at 581.

75. See, for example, *G.C. v. Owensboro Pub. Schs.*, 711 F.3d 623 (6th Cir. 2013).

76. See *In re Gault*, 387 U.S. 1 (1967) (stating that a fifteen-year-old who was committed to a facility for juvenile delinquents had the right to notice of charges, to counsel, to confront and cross-examine witnesses, and to the privilege against self-incrimination).

77. *Goss v. Lopez*, 419 U.S. 565 (1975).

78. *Everett v. Marcase*, 426 F. Supp. 397 (E.D. Pa. 1977).

79. *Hillman v. Elliott*, 436 F. Supp. 812 (W.D. Va. 1977).

80. *Riggan v. Midland Indep. Sch. Dist.*, 86 F. Supp.2d 647 (W.D. Tex. 2000).

81. *Harris ex rel. Harris v. Pontotoc Cnty. Sch. Dist.*, 635 F.3d 685 (5th Cir. 2011)

82. *Nevares v. San Marcos Consol. Indep. Sch. Dist.*, 111 F.3d 25 (5th Cir. 1997).

83. *C.B. By and Through Breeding v. Driscoll*, 82 F.3d 383 (11th Cir. 1996), *reh'g and suggestion for reh'g en banc denied*, 99 F.3d 1157 (11th Cir. 1996).

84. *Buchanan v. City of Bolivar, Tenn.*, 99 F.3d 1352 (6th Cir. 1996).

85. *Lamb v. Panhandle Cmty. Unit Sch. Dist. No. 2*, 826 F.2d 526 (7th Cir. 1987).

86. 424 U.S. 319 (1976).

87. *C.B. By and Through Breeding v. Driscoll*, 82 F.3d 383 (11th Cir. 1996), *reh'g and suggestion for reh'g en banc denied*, 99 F.3d 1157 (11th Cir. 1996).

88. See, for example, *Boykins v. Fairfield Bd. of Educ.*, 492 F.2d 697 (5th Cir. 1974), *cert. denied*, 420 U.S. 962 (1975); *Newsome v. Batavia Local Sch. Dist.*, 842 F.2d 920 (6th Cir. 1988).

89. *Donovan v. Ritchie*, 68 F.3d 14 (1st Cir. 1995).

90. *C.B. By and Through Breeding v. Driscoll*, 82 F.3d 383 (11th Cir. 1996).

91. *L.Q.A. By and Through Arrington v. Eberhart*, 920 F. Supp.1208 (M.D. Ala. 1996), *aff'd without reported opinion*, 111 F.3d 897 (11th Cir. 1997).

92. *Rossi v. West Haven Bd. of Educ.*, 359 F. Supp.2d 178 (D. Conn. 2005).

93. *Newsome v. Batavia Local Sch. Dist.*, 842 F.2d 920 (6th Cir. 1988); *Ruef v. Jordan*, 605 N.Y.S.2d 530 (N.Y. App. Div. 1993).

94. See, for example, *Osteen v. Henley*, 13 F.3d 221 (7th Cir. 1993); *Newsome v. Batavia Local School Dist.*, 842 F.2d 920 (6th Cir. 1988).

95. *In re Expulsion of N.Y.B.*, 750 N.W.2d 318 (Minn. Ct. App. 2008).

96. *Coplin v. Conejo Valley Unified Sch. Dist.*, 903 F. Supp. 1377 (C.D. Cal. 1995), *aff'd in an unpublished opinion*, 116 F.3d 483 (9th Cir. 1997); *Paredes by Koppenhoefer v. Curtis*, 864 F.2d 426 (6th Cir. 1988).

97. *Scanlon v. Las Cruces Pub. Schs.*, 172 P.3d 185 (N.M. Ct. App. 2007); *Newsome v. Batavia Local Sch. Dist.*, 842 F.2d 920 (6th Cir. 1988).

98. *Dillon v. Pulaski Cnty. Special Sch. Dist.*, 468 F. Supp. 54 (E.D. Ark. 1978), *aff'd*, 594 F.2d 699 (8th Cir. 1979); *John A. v. San Bernardino City Unified School Dist.*, 187 Cal.Rptr. 472 (Cal. 1982).

99. *Stinney v. Sumter Sch. Dist. 17*, 707 S.E.2d 397 (S.C. 2011).

100. *Newsome v. Batavia Local Sch. Dist.*, 842 F.2d 920 (6th Cir. 1988).

101. *E.K. v. Stamford Bd. of Educ.*, 557 F. Supp.2d 272 (D. Conn. 2008).

102. *John A. v. San Bernardino City Unified Sch. Dist.*, 187 Cal.Rptr. 472 (Cal. 1982).

103. *J.E. ex rel. Edwards v. Center Moriches Union Free Sch. Dist.*, 898 F. Supp.2d 516, 544 (E.D.N.Y. 2012) (internal citations omitted).

104. See, for example, *Wynar v. Douglas Cnty. Sch. Dist.*, 728 F.3d 1062 (9th Cir. 2013).

105. *Id.* See also *Givens v. Poe*, 346 F. Supp. 202 (W.D.N.C.1972).

106. *Gonzales v. McEuen*, 435 F. Supp. 460 (C.D. Cal. 1977).

107. *Graham v. West Babylon Union Free Sch. Dist.*, 692 N.Y.S.2d 460 (N.Y. App. Div. 1999).

108. *London v. Directors of DeWitt Pub. Schs.*, 194 F.3d 873 (8th Cir. 1999).

109. See also *West v. Derby Unified Sch. Dist. No. 260*, 206 F.3d 1358 (10th Cir. 2000), *cert. denied*, 531 U.S. 825 (2000) (involving a three-day suspension for drawing a Confederate Flag).

110. *Whitfield v. Simpson*, 312 F. Supp. 889 (E.D. Ill. 1970).

111. *Colquitt v. Rich Twp. High Sch. Dist. No. 227*, 699 N.E.2d 1109 (Ill. App. Ct. 1998).

112. *Pierce v. School Comm. of New Bedford*, 322 F. Supp. 957 (D. Mass. 1971).

113. *Nicholas B. v. School Comm. of Worcester*, 587 N.E.2d 211 (Mass. 1992).

114. *Rutz v. Essex Junction Prudential Comm.*, 457 A.2d 1368 (Vt. 1983).

115. *McClain v. Lafayette Cnty. Bd. of Educ.*, 673 F.2d 106 (5th Cir. 1982), *reh'g denied*, 687 F.2d 121 (5th Cir. 1982).

116. *Bystrom By and Through Bystrom v. Fridley High Sch.*, 686 F. Supp. 1387 (D. Minn. 1987), *aff'd without reported opinion*, 855 F.2d 855 (8th Cir. 1988).

117. 484 U.S. 305 (1988).

118. 20 U.S.C.A. §§ 1400 *et seq.*

119. *Honig* at 325.

120. 20 U.S.C.A. §§ 1415(i), (j), (k), (l).

121. 20 U.S.C.A. § 1415(k)(1)(B).

122. 34 C.F.R. § 300.536(a)(1).

123. 34 C.F.R. § 300.536(a)(2).

124. 34 C.F.R. § 300.536(a)(2)(iii).

125. 34 C.F.R. § 300.530(b)(1).

126. 34 C.F.R. § 300.536(b)(2).

127. 20 U.S.C.A. §§ 1415(k)(7)(A), (B).

128. 18 U.S.C.A. § 930(g)(2).

129. 20 U.S.C.A. § 1415(k)(7)(B). For the list of controlled substances, see 21 U.S.C.A. § 812(c).

130. 20 U.S.C.A. § 1415(k)(1)(G)(i).

131. 20 U.S.C.A. § 1415(k)(1)(G)(ii).

132. 20 U.S.C.A. § 1415(k)(1)(C).

133. 20 U.S.C.A. § 1415(k)(1)(G)(iii).

134. 18 U.S.C.A. § 1365(h)(3).

135. 20 U.S.C.A. § 1415(k)(1)(D)(i).

136. 20 U.S.C.A. § 1415(k)(1)(D)(ii).

137. 20 U.S.C.A. § 1415(k)(1)(D)(ii).

138. 20 U.S.C.A. § 1415(k)(1)(D)(ii); 34 C.F.R. § 300.530(d)(ii).

139. 34 C.F.R. § 300.530(f)(1)(ii).

140. 20 U.S.C.A. § 1415(k)(4)(A).

141. 20 U.S.C.A. § 1415(k)(4)(A).

142. 20 U.S.C.A. § 1415(k)(1)(F)(I).

143. See, for example, *School Bd. of Indep. School Dist. No. 11 v. Renollett*, 440 F.3d 1007 (8th Cir. 2006) (explaining that a BIP need not be in writing).

144. 20 U.S.C.A. § 1415(k)(1)(A).

145. 20 U.S.C.A. § 1415(k).

146. 20 U.S.C.A. § 1415(k)(1)(E)(I).

147. 20 U.S.C.A. § 1415(k)(1)(C).

148. 20 U.S.C.A. § 1415(k)(1)(E)(i).

149. 20 U.S.C.A. § 1415(k)(4)(B).

150. 20 U.S.C.A. § 1415(k)(4)(A).

151. 20 U.S.C.A. § 1415(k)(3)(B).

152. *Commonwealth of Va., Dep't of Educ. v. Riley*, 106 F.3d 559 (4th Cir. 1997); *Doe v. Board of Educ. of Oak Park and River Forest High School Dist. 200*,115 F.3d 1273 (7th Cir. 1997), *cert. denied*, 522 U.S. 998 (1997).

153. 20 U.S.C.A. §§ 1412(a)(1)(A), 1415(k)(1)(D)(i).

154. 34 C.F.R. § 300.530(d)(i).

155. 20 U.S.C.A. § 1415(k)(8).

156. 20 U.S.C.A. § 1415(k)(5)(B).

157. 20 U.S.C.A. § 1415(k)(5)(C).

158. 20 U.S.C.A. § 1415(k)(5)(D)(ii).

159. 20 U.S.C.A. § 1415(k)(5)(D)(ii).

160. *Id.*

161. 20 U.S.C.A. § 1415(k)(6)(A).

162. 20 U.S.C.A. § 1415(k)(6)(B).

163. For a comprehensive review of issues dealing with technology in schools, see Osborne and Russo, "Can Students Be Disciplined for Off-campus Cyberspeech."

164. *Lindsey v. Matayoshi*, 950 F. Supp.2d 1159 (D. Hawaii 2013) (upholding a student's expulsion for fighting with a peer and posting comments about it and her opponent on social media).

165. *J.S. v. Bethlehem Area Sch. Dist.*, 807 A.2d 847 (Pa. 2002) (upholding the expulsion of a student who created a Web site, on his own computer while at home containing derogatory remarks about his algebra teacher and asking for collections to pay a hit man to kill the woman).

166. *Layshock ex rel. Layshock v. Hermitage Sch. Dist.*, 650 F.3d 205 (3d Cir. 2011), *cert. denied*, ___ U.S. ___, 132 S. Ct. 1097 (2012) (affirming that educators violated the First Amendment rights of a student who was suspended after using his grandmother's home computer to create a fake internet profile of his principal)

167. *Kowalski v. Berkeley Cnty. Schs.*, 652 F.3d 565 (4th Cir. 2011), *cert. denied*, ___ U.S. ___, 132 S. Ct. 1095 (2012) (upholding a student's suspension for creating and posting to a webpage ridiculing a classmate).

Chapter Six

Reflections and Recommendations

Izak Oosthuizen, Charles J. Russo, and Charl C. Wolhuter

REFLECTIONS

An initial observation gleaned from the chapters in this volume and its companion is that student misconduct presented significant challenges to educators all over the world. Moreover, dealing with learner misbehavior is so complex in its causes that new strategies are needed to address emerging forms of misconduct such as cyber-bullying. At the same time, the difficulties that student misbehavior cause in learning communities undoubtedly come at considerable cost both financially and to all involved.

The forms of student misconduct range dramatically from those that can be described as traditional and minor to those that are increasingly violent. Among the more common forms of misbehavior in just about all of the nations surveyed are students coming to class late, missing classes, leaving school without permission, truancy, improper attire and grooming, cheating on tests or examinations, not handing in work, neglect of academic work, disrespect toward teachers, open defiance and rudeness, forgery, disruptive behavior, obscene language, and using mobile phones without permission.

Serious offenses include fighting/assault, bullying (including cyber-bullying), physical or verbal threats, extortion and intimidation, theft and shoplifting, vandalism, substance abuse, smoking, sexual harassment of teachers or peers, and gang activities. Almost universally, since the use of technology in schools has grown dramatically and shows no signs of slowing down, it presents unique challenges. In fact, the chapters on student discipline in Australia, Singapore, the United Kingdom, and the United States, in varying degrees, identified issues with technology in the form of cyber-bullying and related offenses as an emerging concern.

In the recent past a change has taken place in the conceptualization of the issue of student discipline in schools. To express this phenomenon in Weberian terms in dealing with student discipline, the attitude of educators has evolved from positional to charismatic to rational-legal authority. Further, a discernible international trend evident from the chapters in this volume is the shift toward a creed of human rights forming the parameter for dealing with student misbehavior.

Proponents of the Weberian perspective believe that methods for maintaining learner discipline should be humane. Under this approach, the object of maintaining learner discipline is to create school environments conducive for learning and teaching.

The imperative for sound discipline practices is frequently rooted in National Constitutions and Bills of Human Rights as well as international treaties. Such provisions pertain, for example, to the rights of learners not to be subjected disproportionately to severe treatments or punishment, not to be arrested or detained arbitrarily, and to be treated consistent with the observance of the principles of natural justice.

Student safety and security is a most important reason for a whole set of behavior rules. Under the common law doctrine of *in loco parentis*, literally, "in the place of the parents," educational officials have long had the legal duty to ensure that students are safe while in school. School authorities are thus vested with the power to preserve discipline to protect students, and themselves, from being the victims of misconduct while at the same time ensuring the teaching-learning process continues smoothly.

During the current age of globalization, the human rights base of preserving discipline in schools includes international conventions on Human Rights, such as the 1989 United Nation's Convention on the Rights of the Child,[1] as reflected in its article 37,[2] protecting the child from being punished in cruel or harsh ways. Yet, not all signatories comply with these provisions.

It is exactly this creed of human rights which helped set the tone in the drive to abolish corporal punishment, traditionally one of the main, if not the primary, method of maintaining discipline in schools, in one country after the other. In most of the countries covered in this volume, namely the United Kingdom, most jurisdictions in Australia, most states in the United States, and New Zealand, corporal punishment in schools is illegal.

Common methods used for maintaining discipline in schools can be divided into reactionary and preventative or proactive methods. Reactionary methods include reprimands, oral and written warnings, time-outs, detention, additional school work, informing parents, calling meetings with parents, a points merit-demerit system, taking away of privileges, voluntary withdrawal, disciplinary hearings, and in extreme cases, suspension and expulsions.

Their ultimate disposition is beyond the authority of school officials, but some acts of student misbehavior are referred to the police as criminal acts.

In an item addressed explicitly among the nations reviewed in this volume, only in the United States have courts upheld the exclusion of students who wish to participate in extracurricular activities. American courts agree that students are entitled to less due process to which they might have been entitled to, on the basis that taking part in noneducational or extracurricular activities, most notably sports, are privileges and not rights.

Preventative methods of discipline include having systems of school and classroom rules in place, rewards, and positive discipline. The chapters in the volume reveal a discernible trend of moving toward proactive methods. Interrelated to this trend is the movement to proceeding beyond a tunnel vision of only offenders, whereby educational authorities follow a whole school approach by involving parents, specialist counselors, and members of communities in dealing with learner misconduct in schools.

Part of the trend toward a more humane approach that educators should use when preserving school discipline, especially in keeping with respect for human rights, is that of due process. In this regard, the case with perhaps the most elaborate standards is the U.S. Supreme Court's 1975 decision in *Goss v. Lopez* (*Goss*).[3] *Goss*, which represents the high-water mark of student rights in the United States, has become part of the prescriptive framework for addressing student misconduct, at least in setting broad parameters for students in nations such as Australia, which has a well-developed system in this regard, not just in the United States.

The procedures that the U.S. Supreme Court enunciated in *Goss* are designed to ensure that students receive appropriate due process when they are subject to disciplinary sanctions due to their misbehavior. Following *Goss*, educators in many American schools, and elsewhere such as Australia, provide students, parents, and teachers with opportunities and time to assess and manage their behavior. The United States and Australia also stand out as affording significant due process protections for students with disabilities who face disciplinary sanctions due to the (mis)behaviors.

Educators also seek to offer students the necessary supports to help learners return to school or, in the cases of expulsions, to make other suitable arrangements for them to continue their education. The fundamental principle of natural justice, which is essentially the rights to be heard and to fair and impartial decisions, underpins the procedures in all of the countries reviewed in this volume.

The content of the chapters in this book, coupled with its companion volume and other literature, suggest that research on the effectiveness of methods and strategies to curb student misconduct in order to maintain discipline is scarce. As impressive and praiseworthy as the plans are that were presented in the chapters in this book, they are mainly on the aggregate school level.

Research on student discipline is equally lopsided in favor of school level studies. Unfortunately, as a result of the work in this volume, it is evident that research on the level of what occurs in individual classrooms is sorely lacking. Thus, it would be valuable for a follow-up study to focus on examples dealing with student misconduct on the level of the teachers.

In the international experiences dealing with student discipline surveyed in this book, it is apparent that promising models exist of a restorative nature. These models addressed in this volume are the REACH program in Singapore, and New Zealand's two models in the category of positive discipline approaches, the *Respectful Schools: Restorative Practices in Education* and the *Positive Behavior for Learning Action Plan*. Educators in other nations could fruitfully look to these for guidance.

It is important to keep in mind that the programs briefly described earlier, and throughout this volume, combined with the statutory basis embedded in a human rights culture are indeed indispensable for the creation of an effective teaching and learning environment. However, in many instances this appears to be only one side of the coin.

On the flip side of the proverbial coin, it is equally as important to bear in mind that teaching and learning take place in classrooms, not in courtrooms. Education is essentially a social science founded on the dynamics of sound relationships and mutual respect that must occur in an environment where all share the interest of providing the holistic common good for children.

Against the preceding, it is worth pondering what can be described as the paradoxical nature of learner conduct in some of the modern human rights cultures in the world. On the one hand it is not fair to judge the conduct of all students in leading Western democracies, particularly those reviewed in this volume, by incidents such as when youth looted and burned shops in the United Kingdom or the shootings in Columbine High School in Colorado and in Sandy Hook Elementary School in Newtown, Connecticut, in the United States.

On the other hand, school leaders in China, Malaysia, and Turkey, nations on the edge of human rights practices, and which are reviewed in the companion volume, have relatively few problems with learner misconduct. The chapter on China reports their emphasis on the application of Max Weber's charismatic authority theories instead of the legally regulated approach. In terms of the Weberian perspective, dealings between students and teachers in China are defined in terms of that between a father and son.

The Weberian approach places the emphasis on relationships while elevating the status of the teacher to the respectable role of a parent. This also resonates in the traditional common law, the *in loco parentis* position of the teacher, a notion that seems to have fallen out of fashion in some Western democracies. However, as reflected by the chapter in the companion volume, the *in loco parentis* role of teachers is still strongly emphasized in Malaysia.

The advantage of an emphasis on *in loco parentis* is that it restores the respectful role to the position of teachers while enhancing a kind of intimacy between students and educators. Perhaps the most important aspect thereof is the fact that it restores the traditional role of authority and respect for the teacher in the eyes of the community.

Another key feature of the *in loco parentis* role of teachers is the duty of care, affording educators the obligation, and the authority, to ensure the safety of students. This duty affords teachers the authority to curb student misconduct if needed in order to enforce safe learning environments for all.

When all is said and done, it sometimes seems as if many of the Western countries embedded in a human rights dispensation, are overly focused on the rights of the child. This emphasis was probably enhanced by international law. In this regard one should not underestimate the influence of international law instruments such as the 1989 UN Convention on the Rights of the Child. When compared to the 1959 UN Declaration of the Rights of Child,[4] the former is much more progressive in promoting the individuality and interests of the children.

Surely, there cannot be any argument against the protection of the young and the best interest of the child. Yet, this approach can result in the paradoxical situation whereby it often appears that protecting the rights of students comes at the cost of teachers' status and authority.

The overprotection of students who misbehave is often detrimental to maintaining orderly teaching and learning environments. It could be that the pendulum of caring for student rights versus teacher authority has gone too far to the one side and needs a readjustment. Perhaps educators should seek to balance the scales in terms of affording teachers the authority to discipline learners who misbehave while simultaneously safeguarding student rights. As such, we offer the following recommendations in the hope of promoting discussion about what can work best in practice when safeguarding the rights of all members of school communities.

RECOMMENDATIONS

In light of the preceding analysis, educational leaders and lawyers not only in the nations reviewed in this volume, but elsewhere, should consider the following suggestions as forms of best practice when devising policies and practices addressing learner discipline.

First leaders should ensure that teams charged with developing policies involve representatives of key constituencies, both when they are initially developed and when they are revised because ensuring cooperation is of paramount importance. Policy-writing teams should include members of governing bodies, a school lawyer, administrators, teachers, staff, parents, community members, and learners, particularly at the upper levels since these policies would impact their activities.

Second, policies must include clear, precise definitions of prohibited student behavior such as bullying, intimidation, harassment, and other unacceptable behavior. Insofar as policies mandating punishment for such offenses as acting in a manner that is or saying something "mean" or "hurtful" can easily be invalidated as vague or over-broad, terms must be as precise as possible so that they can survive challenges and help to ensure school safety. Policies should add that off-campus misbehaviors can be punishable if they create hostile environments for victims, infringe on their rights, or create material and substantial disruptions to the educational process in school settings.

Third, policies should forbid physical, verbal, written, and electronic forms of misbehavior that might lead to physical acts of violence or gestures causing physical or emotional harm, damage to the property of victims, place victims in fear of harm, create hostile environments, or infringe on the rights of others.

Fourth, policies should prohibit misbehavior based on race, ethnicity, national origin, socioeconomic status, religion, gender, sexual orientation whether actual or perceived, or disabilities.

Fifth, policies should develop plans to protect victims from retribution and ridicule once they have filed complaints. Taking this step is important because a small, but growing number, of learners have committed suicide in response to being subjected to even more abuse from peers once they reported incidents to educators.

Sixth, policies must include substantive and procedural due process protections that:

a. require students and staff to report instances of disciplinary infractions to designated school officials as soon as reasonably possible after they have occurred, such as by the end of a school day;
b. establish time frames within which administrators must complete investigations, typically ten school days, determining that educators may face liability for deliberate indifference by failing to respond to and investigate incidents;
c. protect the due process rights of the accused since allegations are just that—unless or until they are substantiated, and as such, policies should set deadlines by which time disciplinary processes must be completed, penalties imposed, and appeals filed and resolved while proceedings must be kept confidential;
d. specify a range of penalties for first, second, and repeat offenders from short-term suspensions to expulsions, adding that learners can receive

significant sanctions even on their first offenses—if their actions warrant such discipline; and

e. mandate the reporting of incidents to law enforcement authorities if there is evidence that learners might have committed crimes.

Seventh, policies should be included in student and faculty handbooks. Also, learners and parents should be required to acknowledge in writing that they have read, understood, and agree to abide by these provisions in the handbooks.

Eighth, leaders should provide annual professional development opportunities for dealing with disciplinary problems for teachers and staff.

Ninth, leaders should offer programs for parents to help them better understand and respond to situations in which their children have either misbehaved or been harmed—due to the actions of their peers.

Tenth, leaders should offer counseling to victims and their families to help overcome the effects of being harmed by school violence.

Eleventh, educational leaders should develop peer-intervention or community-based programs such as those addressed in this book to help learners deal with misbehavior and violence in their lives.

Twelfth, teams should review their policies annually and not during or immediately after controversies to ensure that they are up to date with advances in the law, research, and worldview and life-view developments in the societies where they serve.

CONCLUSION

It is a reality of school life that students misbehave with the consequence that their actions often harm peers and ultimately themselves. Educators and lawyers can learn from other nations by identifying guidelines for dealing with similar cases while weighing them against the norms and value systems prevalent in the societies where they serve. Taking such a proactive approach just might help to make schools safe places where learning can actually occur.

NOTES

1. Available at http://www.ohchr.org/EN/ProfessionalInterest/Pages/CRC.aspx
2. This article reads:Article 37
   States Parties shall ensure that:
   (a) No child shall be subjected to torture or other cruel, inhuman or degrading treatment or punishment. Neither capital punishment nor life imprisonment without possibility of release shall be imposed for offences committed by persons below eighteen years of age;

(b) No child shall be deprived of his or her liberty unlawfully or arbitrarily. The arrest, detention or imprisonment of a child shall be in conformity with the law and shall be used only as a measure of last resort and for the shortest appropriate period of time;

(c) Every child deprived of liberty shall be treated with humanity and respect for the inherent dignity of the human person, and in a manner which takes into account the needs of persons of his or her age. In particular, every child deprived of liberty shall be separated from adults unless it is considered in the child's best interest not to do so and shall have the right to maintain contact with his or her family through correspondence and visits, save in exceptional circumstances;

(d) Every child deprived of his or her liberty shall have the right to prompt access to legal and other appropriate assistance, as well as the right to challenge the legality of the deprivation of his or her liberty before a court or other competent, independent and impartial authority, and to a prompt decision on any such action.

Id.

3. 419 U.S. 565 (1975).

4. http://www.un.org/cyberschoolbus/humanrights/resources/child.asp

About the Authors and Editors

Izak Oosthuizen, PhD, taught high school for seventeen years before becoming an associate professor in Education Law on the Potchefstroom campus of the North-West University (NWU) in 1988. In 1999 he was promoted to professor. In 2011 he was appointed as a Research Professor in the Faculty of Education at the NWU Mafikeng campus and in 2014 was named an Extraordinary Professor and Research Specialist. In 2004 Oosthuizen received the Senior Researcher award from the Education Association of South Africa. In 2005 and 2010 he was rated as an established researcher by the NRF. Since 1989 he has published about two hundred book chapters and articles related to education law.

Charles J. Russo, JD, EdD, is the Joseph Panzer Chair in Education in the School of Education and Allied Professions and Adjunct Professor in the School of Law at the University of Dayton, Ohio. The 1998–1999 President of the Education Law Association and 2002 winner of its McGhehey (Lifetime Achievement) Award, he is the author or coauthor of almost 250 articles in peer-reviewed journals and the author, coauthor, editor, or coeditor of fifty-two books. Russo has been the editor of the *Yearbook of Education Law* for the Education Law Association since 1995 and has written or coauthored in excess of 925 publications. He has spoken and taught extensively on issues in education law in the United States and in twenty-six other nations on all six inhabited continents. In recognition of his work in education law, Russo received an honorary PhD from Potchefstroom University, now the Potchefstroom Campus of North-West University, in Potchefstroom, South Africa, in May 2004.

Charl Wolhuter, DEd, is Comparative and International Education Professor at North-West University, Potchefstroom Campus, South Africa. Previously, he taught History of Education and Comparative Education at the University of Pretoria and History of Education and Comparative Education at the University of Zululand. He studied at the Universities of Johannesburg, Pretoria, South Africa, and Stellenbosch; he earned his doctorate in Comparative Education at Stellenbosch. Wolhuter has been guest professor at Brock University, Canada, Canterbury Christ University, United Kingdom, Bowling Green University, and Mount Union University in Ohio, Driestar Pedagogical University, the Netherlands, and the University of Eastern Finland. Wolhuter is the author of books and articles in History of Education and Comparative Education.

Joan Squelch, PhD, is an associate professor and Associate Dean of Teaching and Learning in the School of Law at the University of Notre Dame Australia in Western Australia. Her primary areas of research interest include legal education, legal issues in higher education, workplace bullying, school safety and discipline, and human rights in education.

Mui Kim Teh, PhD, a lawyer and an educator, is a qualified Barrister-at-Law in London, and an Advocate and Solicitor of the Supreme Court of Singapore in 1996. She was a lawyer in Singapore before moving to Australia. Earlier in her career, she was both a teacher and a head of department in Singapore schools. She is the recipient of the inaugural Dr. Ann Shorten Doctoral Thesis Award 2009 given by the Australia and New Zealand Education Law Association for the most outstanding PhD thesis in education law. She is currently based at Deakin University in Victoria, Australia, where she lectures in law.

Sally Varnham, LLM, PhD, is chair of the University Academic Board and Professor with the Faculty of Law at the University of Technology, Sydney. A New Zealander before taking up the position in Australia, she was a Senior Lecturer in the College of Business and a University Proctor at Massey University, Wellington. She has a strong interest in legal issues in education and is the coauthor (with Professor Jim Jackson) of *Law for Educators: School and University Law in Australia*. She was the chief investigator in research projects relating to legal issues in education, most relevantly, the "Student Grievances and Discipline Matters Project" which was funded by a grant from the Australian Learning and Teaching Council. Varnham has published and presented widely in the area of education and the law.

Patricia Walker, PhD, Fellow of the Higher Education Academy, is Visiting Research Fellow in the Cass School of Education and Communities in the University of East London . She has published widely on international education issues in a range of academic journals including, *Journal of Research in International Education*; *Journal of Studies in International Education*; and *Compare*. Walker is a local politician in the London Borough of Ealing where she held the post of Cabinet member for Children and Families for three years before taking up the Cabinet Portfolio for Public Health.

www.ingramcontent.com/pod-product-compliance
Lightning Source LLC
Chambersburg PA
CBHW080426270326
41929CB00018B/3176